These Brothers of Mine

These Brothers of Mine

A Biblical Theology of Land and Family
and a Response to Christian Zionism

ROB DALRYMPLE

WIPF & STOCK · Eugene, Oregon

THESE BROTHERS OF MINE
A Biblical Theology of Land and Family and a Response to Christian Zionism

Wipf & Stock
An Imprint of Wipf and Stock Publishers
199 W. 8th Ave., Suite 3
Eugene, OR 97401

www.wipfandstock.com

ISBN 13: 978-1-4982-0834-5

Manufactured in the U.S.A.   05/07/2015

To my brothers and sisters in Christ throughout the world in general
and the Middle East in particular.
To those in Iraq, Syria, Lebanon, Israel, Jordan, the Palestinian
Territories, Egypt, and beyond.
Especially to our dear friends Kareem and Romana Nino and their
family, Saed Awwad, Salim Munayer, Pastor Evan Thomas, Greg
Khalil, Sami Awad, Alex Awad, Daoud Nassar all those at Bethlehem
Bible College
and all who are suffering for the sake of the kingdom.
We are praying for you.

This book is intended to bring awareness to your plight.
and to help Westerners to realize that our theology may adversely affect
these brothers of mine.

Contents

Preface/Introduction

A new commandment I give to you, that you love one another, even as I have loved you, that you also love one another. By this all men will know that you are My disciples, if you have love for one another.

JOHN 13:34–35

This book has been extremely difficult to write. I am pretty confident that I have deleted more pages than I have included in the final version of this book. My great concern throughout has been trying to relay my thesis without being misunderstood. I know that what I have to say here does not correlate well with much of contemporary evangelical thinking. I am convinced that what I have spelled out here is quite in line with Scripture. However, I know that some will disagree. The problem is that when we disagree with others we tend to misread them. Not necessarily intentionally. So, I struggled to make sure that I was saying what I wanted to say with enough clarity to eliminate, or at least minimize, misunderstandings.

My thesis is simple: Jesus is the fulfillment of all God's promises. I have found in my years of teaching and preaching that many Christians simply have too low a view of Jesus. The implications are significant: the people of God in the New Testament world are comprised of those from every nation and, as such, we are not to give allegiance to any one nation as superior to another, but to the people of God ("These Brothers of Mine") who dwell in all the nations.

I previously held to a theology that favored one nation (Israel). And I opposed those nations who opposed it. I do think that this thinking, which is prevalent among many Western Christians, has not helped to create peace, either for Israel, or for the nations. In fact, it has at times encouraged conflict.

Since we follow the Prince of Peace it is time for voices of peace to speak up. I do so with the full intent of affirming all peoples. We love the Jewish people. We love the Arab world. We love all men. And most of all, we love one another!

Rob Dalrymple
October 2014

Acknowledgments

There have been many people who have helped in the writing of this book. Without their tireless efforts I am not sure this project would ever have been completed. This book would not be much without the tireless work of Ian Spencer. Ian spent countless hours rereading and editing several versions of this book. His knowledge and expertise with the English language are only surpassed by his humility. I cannot thank him enough. Vanessa Barditzky was also very helpful in editing many of the early drafts of this book. She was brave enough to read it when it was not very good. If it has turned out well, it is largely due to her help.

I would also like to thank the many others who read and commented on this manuscript at its various stages: including my son Justin Dalrymple, my brother Bill Dalrymple, Greg Khalil, Fr. Leo Arrowsmith, Derry Calay, Tom Biesiada, Carol Dent, and Vinnie Angelo. Without their help this whole book would be in the trash instead of just half of it!

Part 1

Foundations

Chapter 1

Why Discuss Christian Zionism?[1]

Open your mouth, judge righteously, and defend the rights of the afflicted and needy.

—Proverbs 31:9

A 2013 Pew survey found that 82 percent of Evangelicals believe that Israel was given to the Jewish people by God.[2]

The King will answer and say to them, "Truly I say to you, to the extent that you did it to one of these brothers of Mine, even the least of them, you did it to Me."

—Matthew 25:40

I am quite aware that the topic of "Israel" among many Christians is explosive and that writing a book on Christian Zionism is like venturing into

---

1. Christian Zionism is, simply put, the belief that the promises to Abraham that God would give his descendants the Holy Land must be fulfilled by physical/ethnic Israelites. For a discussion, see chaps. 10–14.

2. Cited in Jonathan Mark, "Evangelicals at the Crossroads," *Jewish Week*, February 19, 2014, http://www.thejewishweek.com/news/national/evangelicals-crossroads.

a minefield. But I am convinced that this is a minefield into which we must enter. The church must listen.

Some may even question as to why we should even care about a conflict in the Middle East. For one, we must understand that the people of God have been called for a mission. Our mission is to be the hands and feet of Christ as he works to establish his kingdom. We are to be the light of the world.[3] A light that brings truth, peace, and justice to all of God's creation.[4]

Furthermore, we care because people matter to God: Israelis and Palestinians; Jews and Arabs. All people matter to God. Therefore, they must matter to the people of God also.

In addition, we care because there are Christians in this land. There is a struggling, yet burgeoning, church growing in Israel. Within Palestine, the church, which has existed since the time of Christ,[5] is suffering and dying. One of the most overwhelming things I have heard—and I have heard it many times—is when I ask Christians in these regions what they would like me to tell the church in the West about their current plight and they reply, "Just tell them that we are here."

Why does the conflict in the Holy Land matter to us? For many reasons. One of which is that Jesus said whatever we do to "the least of these brothers of Mine" we do to him (Matt 25:40).[6] The reality is that Western theology has served to encourage a conflict in the Holy Land that has adversely affected many, including our brothers and sisters in Christ.[7]

3. Cf. Isa 42:6; 49:6; Matt 5:14–16.

4. This was a major thesis of my book *Understanding Eschatology*, which in many ways is a prequel to the present book.

5. It should be noted that according to Acts 2:9–11 there were "Arabs" at Pentecost. Furthermore, we may assume that some of the first Jewish converts to Christianity in Acts soon began to intermarry with those of non-Jewish descent. These early Christians were then assimilated racially into what became the Palestinian culture over the next few centuries. As a result, some of the present day Palestinians may well be descended from these first Christians.

6. All translations, unless otherwise indicated are from the NASB. I will argue at length in chap. 15 that "these brothers of Mine" (my own translation) are followers of Christ.

7. What I mean here is that the conviction that the Holy Land belongs to the Jewish people, which is a common conviction among evangelicals, has contributed to the conviction that we (the United States and Britain in particular) must support Israel. Knowing that a large contingency of evangelical voters will support US foreign policy in support of Israel has contributed to the conflict in the Holy Land. The problem, which many evangelicals are simply unaware of, is that the Christian community in Palestine has suffered as a result of the occupation of the West Bank and Gaza. Note: I am not

So this book indeed brings us to a minefield. A minefield of Christian beliefs. On the one hand, we have Christian Zionists,[8] who are often sincere, Bible-believing Christians that are deeply convinced that the Bible makes definitive claims that the Holy Land[9] belongs to the Jewish people. Christian Zionists have a strong conviction that the only way to read the Bible is "literally." They contend that the Bible clearly predicts that the Jewish people will return to their historic homeland and many believe that the events of 1948 and 1967 are the fulfillment of those promises.[10] According to Christian Zionists, to read the Bible any other way is to "spiritualize" the Bible and renders the meaning of the Bible subjective and open to radical interpretations. Anyone who might question the Christian Zionist reading (in particular, the view that the promises of land to Abraham must be fulfilled by the physical descendants of Abraham) is immediately suspected of holding to a liberal reading of the Bible. They conclude that to support the modern state of Israel is to support God.[11]

---

saying that the United States and Britain should not support Israel or that Israel is bad. I am simply noting that Christians in the West have created a situation in which, as a result of their zeal to support Israel, they have increased the suffering of "these brothers of mine."

8. I will define and discuss Christian Zionism much more thoroughly in part 3 (chaps. 9–14) of this book.

9. The problem of language will confront us on virtually every page of this book. For many of the terms referring to the people and the land are highly charged. When it comes to the land do we call it "Palestine," which is a common designation used by the scholarly community and which takes its name from the Roman designation of the area in AD 135? The problem here is that "Palestine" is the preferred title of the Palestinian community, yet it is rejected by the Israelis. Do we call the land "Judea and Samaria," which is the preferred title of the Israelis? The problem here is that it is used to substantiate the claim that the land belongs to the Jewish descendants of the ancient Israelites to the neglect of the present day Palestinians. And the list goes on. I will prefer the title "Holy Land" since the people of all three of the great religions (Christianity, Judaism, and Islam) acknowledge a sacredness to the land. I will not, however, attempt to delineate the borders of the Holy Land. On occasion, I will refer to it as "the Promised Land." I will use this title when referring to the promise of land to Abraham (Gen 15:7).

10. This is a prevalent view among popular-level evangelicals. I have had numerous conversations with parishioners who will not accept the biblical evidence that certain prophecies are to be understood as fulfilled in the New Testament (NT) because they are convinced that they were fulfilled in 1948. Christian Zionist publications are more reticent to hail 1948 and 1967 as fulfillments of prophecy because they understand that Israel has not returned spiritually to the Lord.

11. Sandra Teplinsky states, "Ultimately, how a person treats the Jews will reveal whether or not he is saved" (*Why Care about Israel*, 20). Teplinsky is citing the NIV Study Bible here (see NIV Study Bible, note on Matt 25:31–46.) Unfortunately, the NIV

On the other hand,[12] many equally sincere Christians[13] are convinced that the promises to Abraham of family (descendants as numerous as the stars) and land (the Holy Land) are fulfilled in Jesus. They reject the claim that the Holy Land necessarily belongs exclusively to the physical descendants of Abraham. As a result, they reject the claim that 1948 and 1967 were a fulfillment of prophecy.

And so we have two sides—with others in between. Each tries to trump the views of the other: sometimes asserting a particular view of Scripture; other times citing the injustices of the modern conflict. Caught in the middle are people: Israelis and Palestinians; moms and dads; brothers and sisters; sons and daughters. People who simply want to live alongside their neighbors in peace.[14] They want their kids to go to school, get a good job, find a spouse, and raise a family without the fear of bombings or the constant threat of terror. We must ever be reminded that it is *people* who are caught in the middle of this conflict that has been brewing for more than half a century.[15]

Study Bible note was not asserting this as true. Instead, the note was merely listing some of the more common positions of interpretation with regard to this verse (even then the NIV note only listed two out of the several views of interpretation on this passage—see chap. 17 of this book for a more detailed discussion). In her footnotes Teplinsky acknowledges, "The NIV note (correctly, in my opinion) does not limit the interpretation of 'these brothers of mine' to only the Jewish people" (255n1). The problem is that this is not what her main text leads the reader to believe.

12. There are, of course, more than two views. I am merely presenting the poles of belief.

13. I must note here that many of those who advocate for the following view are indeed equally sincere Christians. I say this because the tradition in which I personally was raised would strongly question whether or not these people ("liberals," as we knew them) are sincere followers of Jesus. In fact, I recently had a conversation with someone who still adheres to this thinking. I shared with him the plight of Christians in the Middle East. I was shocked, though I am not sure why I was shocked, when he replied, "I am not sure that the people we are talking about are Christians."

14. I realize that some readers have a predisposition to reject this. It is commonly asserted that one side in this conflict wants nothing more than the eradication of the other. Though this may be true among some radicals, my response is simple: have you ever sat with these people? Have you spent a day with them? Have you taken a walk, or had a cup of coffee with them? Sure there are radicals on every side. But the common folk, they are just like most of us.

15. It is simply not true to suggest that this conflict has been raging since the time of Ishmael and Isaac. Unfortunately, this popular myth has been perpetuated all too often. This myth is one of the main points in Bryant Wright's book *Seeds of Turmoil*. Wright claims, "The seeds of turmoil of this sibling rivalry began with their (Ishmael and Isaac's)

As with any minefield, I intend to tread lightly and I ask for grace. I enter because I believe that the Lord wills us to speak truth when there is error. If, in the end, we disagree on the theological side, so be it. We must, however, find common ground on the ethical side. Terrorist bombings must end; confiscations of land must end; needless imprisonments and the deaths of children must end. Peace must reign.

To side with Israel against the Palestinians, or the Palestinians against Israel, is not to stand with Jesus. The kingdom that Jesus established transcends racial and nationalistic boundaries. The people of God must advocate for peace and the human dignity of all people (Jews, Muslims, Christians, and any others). We must renounce terrorism and the oppression of any people, regardless of who the perpetrator is.

In saying this, I fully recognize that many Christians have a deeply-rooted understanding of Scripture that they believe requires them to advocate for Israel. This book is an attempt to address the theological issues of temple, family (who are the chosen people and the true heirs of Abraham) and land (what does the Bible say about the promise of land to Abraham and his descendants).

The fear is that in responding to Christian Zionism, many will immediately assume that I am arguing for the opposite.[16] I am not. I am not advocating for any side in the complex battles that ravage this land. I am merely writing a biblical theological book that examines God's promises of family and land in Scripture. I am not, however, addressing in any manner the complex political and social issues surrounding the Holy Land today. I will leave that for people far more qualified than me.

If I could offer any input on the role of the people of God in matters such as these it would be that we should reflect the exhortation of Christ: "Blessed are the peacemakers" (Matt 5:9).[17]

---

conception" (54).

16. The assertion that anyone who argues against Christian Zionism is anti-Jewish is the basis of Barry Horner's polemical book *Future Israel: Why Christian Anti-Judaism Must Be Challenged*. The subtitle says it all. Horner describes anyone who holds the view that God's promises to Israel are fulfilled in Jesus as anti-Jewish. This is a shame.

17. I have had many object to the assertion that we should endorse peace by commenting that there is a time for war. My response (which transcends the focus of this book, so I will be brief) is that the NT people of God are never called to advocate for war beyond the spiritual battle we face with the devil.

Chapter 2

Avoiding Theological Merry-Go-Rounds

Merry-go-rounds. They are an integral part of playgrounds everywhere. Something to be enjoyed by children. But they have no place in theological discussions. Unfortunately, however, they are all too common in theological debates. What do I mean?

Have you ever engaged someone in a theological debate only to realize, sometimes hours later, that you are discussing the same points that were raised an hour earlier? You had cited a verse or passage that "clearly" proved your position only to be rebutted by your friend who cited their own verse, which just as "clearly" countered your verse and somehow supported their position. As the conversation continued, the debate continued in this manner. Each side cited verses that rebutted the other's view and supported their own. After some time you realize that you and your partner in dialogue were restating the same points that had been made an hour earlier. "Why," you think to yourself, "are they bringing up that verse again? I already answered them on that point." No matter what you seem to say they have a counter—often the same one they gave you an hour ago. And the merry-go-round continues.

Now merry-go-rounds may be great fun for children in the park, but they are not enjoyable when they are experienced as part of a theological conversation. The problem is that such conversations rarely bear much fruit. At the end of the day, each side walks away frustrated. Frustrated because the other person did not listen well enough. Frustrated because they did not really understand. Many are often so wounded by such conversations that they refuse to partake of them in the future. Families are divided. Friendships are lost. Churches are split.

The difficulty, which at times even trained theologians fail to comprehend, stems from the fact that each side in the discussion approaches the biblical text with their own assumptions. These assumptions, which everyone has, radically affect the way we read the biblical text. Unless we address the discussion at the level of our assumptions we will never proceed very far in such conversations.

A merry-go-round, after all, only appears to take you somewhere. It is not long until you realize that for all the time you have spent on the playground, you have simply arrived at the very place from which you set out.

ADDRESSING THESE MATTERS FROM SCRIPTURE

How do we avoid a merry-go-round debate? The solution is found by discovering our assumptions and those of our opponent. From here the conversation must attempt to address which set of assumptions makes the most sense of the entire biblical story.[1] To do so we must be willing to set our assumptions on the table and to honestly evaluate them.[2] Otherwise, we will simply have to enjoy the theological merry-go-round.

1. One of the problems in theological discussions today is that many are ill-equipped to debate a passage in light of the whole of the biblical story. Many do not know the whole of the biblical story. They may know many individual stories, or some of them, but how the Scriptures weave these stories into one large narrative is missing for many Christians. Since many are not familiar enough with the whole of the biblical story, we must proceed with caution when it comes to interpreting the Bible.

2. A conviction that should be held by all Christians is that we should always be willing to put our assumptions on the table in order to discern if they are correct. This is an essential step in healthy dialogue and is critical for Christians as we grow in the likeness of Christ. For one, our willingness to honestly evaluate the legitimacy of our own beliefs demonstrates that we are people of integrity. This will gain us much respect in the eyes of the person with whom we are debating—whether they are a brother or sister in Christ or not. After all, if we are asking the person with whom we are debating to put their assumptions on the table, then we ought to be willing to put ours on the table as well. Also, as followers of Christ we have nothing to fear. If Christ is the Truth and all truth leads to him, then we should be more than willing to put our assumptions and our convictions on the table to discern if they are legitimate. For if our assumptions in a particular instance are not true, then our beliefs that arise from these assumptions may well be leading us away from the truth and thereby away from Christ. We should want to know where we are mistaken so that we may be corrected in order that we may conform our beliefs to the truth, and, consequently, toward Christ. This also means that we must be willing to admit when we are wrong. Ideally, we should be willing to swallow our pride and admit our error if needed in order to be more in line with the truth that is Christ. As Christians, we should be the most open-minded of all people. For we have nothing to fear (cf. 1 John

At this point, I would like to add a caveat or two. I realize that many readers are ready to dig in and defend their beliefs at all costs on these matters. I respect that we have strongly held convictions on such issues. And, at the end of the day, if my interpretation of Scripture is not convincing to you, so be it. But I would like to note that we cannot simply overlook one important fact: God loves all people and so should we. We must not demonize those on the other side simply because we disagree them. We must not make all Israelis or all Palestinians bad people. We must care for everyone in this conflict. That is what it means to be peacemakers.

One of the difficulties in advocating for peace in the Holy Land is that many within popular Western Christianity actually advocate for war.[3] Some do so on the basis that war in this region is inevitable.[4] After all, they suppose, war has been going on in the Holy Land since the time of Isaac and Ishmael.[5] Others contend that war is a sign of the imminent return of Christ.

This creates a conundrum. On the one hand, we are called to be peacemakers (Matt 5:9). Yet, on the other hand, many are advocating for war. Those who do the latter attempt to justify their position by their theological convictions regarding the promises of family and land to Abraham. Many within this camp suggest that the Jewish people have an absolute right to

---

4:18: "There is no fear in love"). After all, all truth leads to Christ.

Admittedly, this is not easy to do. The fact is that there is great diversity even among trained theologians. This diversity should teach us many things. For one, it should teach us that some things may be beyond our ability to grasp fully. In such matters we must be willing to allow grace to reign. Sometimes this diversity can be accounted for by the fact that not even trained scholars are fully aware of the assumptions to which they adhere. On other occasions, we must admit that even theologians, pastors, and leaders are at times unwilling to admit that they are mistaken. This is a shame.

3. John Hagee, who may have one of the largest pro-Israel movements in evangelical Christianity, specifically advocates for war in his writings and teachings. See the video posted by the pro-peace organization WHTT (We Hold These Truths) in which Hagee prays for war in the Holy Land, http://vimeo.com/34409225. See also the July 11, 2014, article in *Mondoweiss* titled, "Israeli Ambassador Ron Dermer Gives Pro-War Pep Talk to Christian Zionists," http://mondoweiss.net/2014/07/ambassador-christian-zionists.html.

4. Bryant Wright's book *Seeds of Turmoil* has the subtitle *The Biblical Roots of the Inevitable War in the Middle East*. The problem with this thinking is that it makes many apathetic to war. There is no need to strive for peace if war is inevitable!

5. This claim is simply not true. See chap. 1 n14.

the Holy Land and that Christians must support them in order to receive the blessings of God.[6]

THESIS: GOD'S PROMISES ARE FULFILLED IN JESUS

In the central part of this book, chapters 4 through 8, I will present what I believe is the proper theological foundation for understanding Scripture in general, as well as for understanding the promises of family and land to Abraham. That foundation is Jesus.[7] I will argue that all of God's promises are fulfilled in Jesus (2 Cor 1:20). Christ is the proper foundation for understanding all of Scripture. That is, Jesus is the fulfillment of the temple. He *is* the temple. In addition, we will see that the promises to Abraham that his descendants would be as numerous as the stars of the sky and sand on the seashore[8] and the promise that God has given the Holy Land to Abraham and his descendants[9] are also fulfilled in Jesus. Jesus is the true descendant of Abraham and the one through whom the promises are fulfilled. The promises of family and land to Abraham were fulfilled by Jesus. Therefore, though we love the Jewish people, we are not awaiting some miraculous restoration of Abraham's physical offspring to the land as though it were the fulfillment of biblical prophecy.

The primary objective of this book is to provide a foundation for understanding the biblical worldview regarding family and land. In part 3, I will then respond to the common objections to my viewpoint set forth by Christian Zionists. For example, I will address the criticism that my position represents Replacement Theology,[10] the charge that the promises of family and land to Abraham were unconditional promises that must be fulfilled exclusively by the physical/ethnic descendants of Abraham, and the claim that the restoration of Israel as a nation in 1948 was a fulfillment of prophecy.

6. See the June 12, 2009, article on the NPR website, "American Christian Funding Flows to Jewish Settlers," http://www.npr.org/templates/story/story.php?storyId=105310088.

7. This is the major premise in my book *Understanding Eschatology*.

8. Cf. Gen 15:5; 22:17; 26:4; 32:12.

9. Cf. Gen 15:7, 18; 17:8.

10. Does it? Simply put, the answer is no. For a more thorough response, as well as a description of what Replacement Theology is, see chap. 11. In fact, I will argue in chap. 11 that Replacement Theology has the same fundamental flaws inherent in Christian Zionism.

In the final section of this book (part 4), I will address the Parable of the Sheep and the Goats in Matthew 25:31–46. I believe that this parable speaks to the church in regard to our responsibility to care for one another. I will argue that "these brothers of mine" are defined in Matthew's gospel as those who follow Christ.[11] This is the point at which a theological debate has become a matter of great concern. For all the bantering as to who owns the land and what the Bible promises must occur before the return of Christ, we must realize that real people are caught in the middle of a full-blown global crisis. Add to this that our theological opinions may well be contributing to the suffering of "these brothers of mine" and we soon realize that the church in the West can no longer be silent. "You did it to Me" (Matt 25:40).

Ultimately, this book is about people. Though it may stress a biblical understanding of family and land, this book is about people. In a sense it is about the fundamental dignity of all people. The problem that this book aims to address is the fact that many Christians have embraced a theological position, called Christian Zionism, which predisposes them to support one side over against the other. The tragedy is that in the end both sides are suffering.

11. See chap. 17.

Chapter 3

My Story[1]

I was raised in a very conservative, evangelical world. The Bible was plenty clear for us in numerous, if not all, matters. When it came to understanding Israel, the land, and prophecy it was quite plain.

I considered Israel's restoration to the land in the twentieth century—in particular the events of 1948 and 1967—as clear evidence of the fulfillment of prophecy. I championed the views of Hal Lindsay, Grant Jeffrey, and the whole "Left Behind" world. The return of the Jews and the establishment of Israel was not only a fulfillment of prophecy, but was prima facie evidence that Jesus was returning soon.

When it came to the Palestinians, I had very little awareness. I only "knew" that the land belonged to Israel and if the Palestinians were in the way, that was ultimately their problem. I was convinced that just as Joshua had expelled the Canaanites so, also, modern Israel had every right to expel the Palestinians. This was the Jewish people's land. God had given it to them. And I did not think to question this.

As for the present crisis, I honestly knew very little. I assumed that all Palestinians were Muslims—though honestly at the time I am not sure that I even knew what a Palestinian was. I had never heard of an Israeli settlement. I had no idea what an intifada was. I barely knew what the West Bank was. American television, which I rarely tuned into, had made me

1. The following story relates my own personal experiences. In many ways it is central to this book. It relates not only who I am and from where I have come, but also why I believe that we must think more deeply about these issues. For an audio presentation of this chapter, see my website, http://determinetruth.com/media/listen, and click on "Rob's Bio."

somewhat aware of the appalling terror attacks against the Israelis. It made sense that Israel would do everything possible to protect itself. I understood that within years of the horror of the Holocaust the Jewish people were able to secure a homeland for themselves back in the land that God had given to Abraham millennia ago.

Then I traveled to the land myself. Suddenly, I began to sense that something was amiss. I began to realize that there was more to the story.

MY FIRST TRIP TO THE HOLY LAND: 2003

My first experience in the Holy Land came in 2003. I had enrolled in a two week graduate intensive course at a Christian university in Jerusalem. It was a great experience. I was walking where Jesus walked! Little did I know that two innocent events would be the basis for launching me into a deeper exploration of the biblical and theological questions of family and land.

My first experience might well seem benign. I had opted to take part in a three-day excursion to Jordan before the formal start of the actual course. It was a wonderful and enriching experience. On our way back to Jerusalem from Jordan, we proceeded to return to Jerusalem via the Allenby crossing. It was later that I came to learn that the Allenby crossing from Jordan into the West Bank was the one place through which Palestinians who had crossed into Jordan were allowed to return.

As we approached the checkpoint, our leader informed us that we needed to hurry as it was getting late (as I recall it was maybe as late as 3:00 in the afternoon) and the crossing was going to close soon. As we entered the building where we would later be searched and our passports examined, I remember someone telling me that the women and children who were huddled throughout the building had been waiting here all day. I immediately thought to myself that because we were Americans with US passports we would get through quite quickly. And we did. Though it did take almost two hours. I also knew in my heart that there was something unfair and unjust for these women and children, who were obviously Palestinians (I realize now of course that they were Palestinians; at the time I would have thought of them only as Muslims as a result of the head coverings and modest clothing), to have to wait all day. And I felt sorry for them.[2]

2. I recognize, of course, that the issue is very complex. Israel has legitimate security needs and the Palestinians are perceived as a threat to their existence. The problem is that these Palestinians were not attempting to cross from Jordan to Israel. The Allenby

After a thorough examination by the Israeli soldiers, we were allowed to continue on our journey. We returned to Jerusalem safely. The next day class began. The thought of these women and children being forced to wait slipped my mind. It was only several years later that I realized that this seemingly innocuous event had stayed with me.

My second experience occurred a week later. It was Sunday morning. We were halfway through our two-week course. Being that it was Sunday, we were given the morning off from class in order to attend church and rest. During the previous week, my instructor had encouraged us to venture over to Bethany in our free time. Bethany was the place of Lazarus' tomb and other sites, which we were not going to experience as part of the course. The prospect of traveling from Bethany, the town where Jesus may have spent the last week of his life, to Jerusalem just as Jesus did excited me.

I was able to encourage a younger classmate to travel with me. As we prepared to head out on the two mile journey we were informed that we might need our passports. This caused us some concern. Why would we need our passports? Was it safe in Bethany? I elected to take my passport, but no money. The young man who traveled with me informed me that he had his passport and a $20 bill.

Because we did not know precisely where we were going, let alone how to get there (beyond the general sense that it was east of Jerusalem and somewhat around the Mount of Olives), we wandered a bit. We must have looked lost.

Soon an Israeli military jeep pulled up alongside us and a young Israeli soldier peered out his window and asked us where we were heading. This was a moment of great tension. We did not think we were doing anything wrong, but all of a sudden we were not sure. I replied, hesitatingly, that we were trying to go to Bethany. The soldier immediately explained that if we went three blocks up the hill there would be a place to cross on the right. So we continued on with some measure of confidence that our journey was acceptable.

As we approached the place where the soldier had informed us that we would be able to cross, we came across a makeshift barrier blocking the middle of the street. However, at the point in which this barrier and the property fence on the side of the road met people were squeezing around

---

crossing was granting Palestinians access to the Palestinian territories. That is, many of them were returning to their homes in the West Bank. To detain them all day and hinder them from returning to their homes did not sit well with me.

the barrier by climbing upon debris that had been piled up in order to cross from one side to another. The amazing part of it all was that an Israeli soldier with an Uzi was helping people across.

In light of the fact that an Israeli soldier had just informed us where to cross and that another Israeli soldier was assisting dozens of people around this barrier, we figured that we were okay to cross too. Nonetheless, the young man and I were both apprehensive.

Once we crossed to the other side of the barrier we were even more afraid. I suddenly thought to myself that I was safe in Israel. After all, I was an American. America is an ally of Israel. But, I thought to myself, I was not safe here (wherever "here" was). A glance at my young friend confirmed that he too was visibly nervous.

We walked a short distance up the road to the crest of a hill. The young man then asked where I thought we should go (no one had told us where Lazarus' tomb was; we were only told that it was in Bethany). As I nervously looked around, I suddenly noticed that directly below where we were standing was a church. I blurted quite suddenly, "Let's go there!" Surely we would be safe in a church!

It was Sunday and a very small service was already underway. Since the service was not in English (Arabic I now presume), we had no idea what was happening. Besides, we had already been to a morning service. So, we remained for only a few minutes and then departed.

We proceeded down a moderately narrow street to the east. After walking no more than a few blocks, I suddenly looked up and noticed a sign above a large metal door with a padlock. To our amazement the sign said: "Lazarus' tomb." We found it! We may not have known where it was, but we found it.

Across the narrow street no more than twenty feet away were two Arab gentlemen. One of them asked, in somewhat broken English, "Do you want in?" We both agreed and replied, "Sure"—after all, that is why we journeyed here.

The man then went into his house and retrieved some keys. After opening the door, we noticed a spiral stairway that descended to a cave. True story here: I was so nervous (I honestly had thoughts of two American men being trapped in a cave never to be heard from again) that I told the young man, "You go first; I'll wait here."

The young man went down. After taking some time looking around, he returned to the street. So, with a great measure of trepidation, I wandered in. As I went down the stairs, I thought to myself, "A cave is a cave." So, I only went about two-thirds of the way down, peered around the stairs to look at the cave, and quickly exited.

As I came out of the cave, the man who had opened the door then said with a thick Palestinian accent, "That will be four shekels each" (two dollars!). I gasped because I had no money! The young man then immediately pulled out his $20 bill and exclaimed, "All I have is a twenty dollar bill." I thought to myself at once, "This poor kid. He just lost $20." Incredulously, however, the man responded, "No problem. I make change." He took the $20 and went into his house for what must have been a good five minutes.

We proceeded to have a pleasurable conversation with the other Arab gentleman on the porch—despite the fact that his English skills were not as good. After five minutes or so, the man came out and exclaimed, "Okay. I have $8 in shekels, and $10 in American money." I was flabbergasted. He had clearly searched for some time to find this money. But, I thought to myself, "The man could have lied." He could have said he only found $2 and pocketed an additional $16. And there would have been nothing we could have done about it. But that is not what he did. He searched hard to find us change.

Suddenly my world was spinning. It seemed as though everything I had been told was being undermined. We were supposed to be scared. These people were terrorists. They were our enemies. Yet, we had just left a church. Now we have met two gentlemen who were some of the nicest people you would ever meet.

The young man and I proceeded to walk down the street another block or so. Looking ahead a short distance, I saw a sign over the entrance to a courtyard that read: "Oldest house in Palestine." A gentlemen stood in the doorway and very excitedly encouraged us to come in and see what a first-century home looked like. "Just like the one that Mary and Martha and Lazarus lived in," he excitedly proclaimed. As I peered through the entrance, I saw a small bowl with a sign saying, "Donations welcome." I immediately realized that this man was not about to rip us off. Plus, my young associate had change! So we entered and were treated by a cheerful, gracious host to a beautiful tour of his home!

Part 1: Foundations

What Was I to Do with All This?

I returned to Jerusalem that day and then later to the States. I honestly did not think much about my experiences. I was just beginning to write my dissertation and had little time or energy to continue this journey. These two events, however, stuck with me.

I had seen what appeared to be injustice at the Allenby crossing. Women and children that we not being treated fairly. I had met some Palestinians and found them to be honest and kind. And, to my surprise, some of them were Christians.[3] These memories were to be filed in the back of my mind only to be retrieved several years later.

MY RETURN TO THE LAND IN 2008

Five years later I returned to the Holy Land escorting a group of students from my local church. This time the Lord caused me to see much more.

Midway through this trip our group traveled by bus to Bethlehem. I had been to Bethlehem five years earlier. During my first trip to Bethlehem in 2003, I recall being warned that Bethlehem was not a safe place (the second intifada had just ended). We were told that we should proceed from the bus depot to the Church of the Nativity and back without interacting with the locals. We were not to buy water or souvenirs, or even to speak with the locals.

This time, during our bus ride to Bethlehem I began to sense that the drive was taking much longer than it should have. After all, Bethlehem is only about five miles southwest of Jerusalem. I peered out the window of the bus to see where we might be. I immediately recognized Bethlehem directly to the east. But, for some reason our bus was taking us around Bethlehem to the west. I then inquired of the person across the aisle from me—to this day, I do not remember who this person was[4]—why we were traveling around Bethlehem.

It was explained to me that we were traveling on a new bypass highway. "What's a 'bypass' highway?" I asked. This mysterious person then

3. I realized later that I had just assumed that when Islam invaded this land in the seventh century they eliminated all the Christians; little did I know that Christians, Jews, and Muslims had lived together as neighbors in this land for hundreds of years.

4. Our group was not large enough to fill the entire class for this trip, so we were joined with at least one other group from the states.

explained that the bypass highways were built so that Israeli settlers could travel from their settlements to Jerusalem without having to travel through Bethlehem or other Palestinian cities.

This explanation was not helpful either. For I had no idea what a settler was.[5] This person proceeded to explain to me that settlers were Jewish Israelis who lived in the West Bank—that is, they are Jewish people who live in the Palestinian Territories (whole cities have been erected throughout the West Bank in order to accommodate Jewish settlers).[6] This person further explained that some of the most violent clashes among the Jews and the Palestinians occurred when the settlers drove from their settlements through Palestinian cities en route to Jerusalem and other locations. This new highway was built so that the settlers could travel around, instead of through, Palestinian cities. (I don't recall if I learned then or later that such highways, which are built one hundred percent on Palestinian lands, are not open for use by the Palestinians. In fact there are different license plates that identify Israeli cars and Palestinian cars). I thought to myself that this did not seem right.

Within moments of this conversation I proceeded to look out the window again. By now Bethlehem was completely in view from the West. This time I noticed a large concrete wall was placed at the edge of the city. The wall, which was (and still is) under construction, was pushed up against the city of Bethlehem itself, while the orchards and olive groves belonging to the residents of Bethlehem lay outside the wall. I did not understand why Israel was building a wall around Bethlehem. So I inquired of my personal informant. I was told that the wall was built by Israel as a security fence to keep suicide bombers from getting out.[7] This made some sense.

But I knew in my heart that this was not all right. The wall and the bypass highway seemed unjust. Taking land from families—land that in some cases had been passed down for centuries—and building a highway for illegal residents,[8] with the effect of cutting a city and its people off from

5. I am amazed to learn that most of the people in churches across the United States that I share this story with have no idea what a settlement is either.

6. There are now more than five hundred thousand Israeli citizens who live in the West Bank.

7. This wall is termed a "separation barrier" by the Israelis. Since the construction of the barrier began in 2002, there has indeed been a dramatic reduction in terrorism.

8. The presence of Jewish settlers in the West Bank is illegal by international law and is a major issue when it comes to establishing peace in the land. I realize that some readers may claim that God has given this land to the Jewish people. I will address the

their own orchards and olive groves must be a great hardship to the people. If people cannot work their own land, then the economic hardship must be severe. If people cannot leave their own city for work (only a small percentage of the residents of Bethlehem are still permitted to leave the city for employment), this too would further cripple the economy. In addition, if the residents of Bethlehem are imprisoned within their own city, the psychological and sociological impact must be great.

As the bus continued, we entered Bethlehem from the south. I noticed that we did not go through any wall—meaning that the wall did not circumnavigate the entire city. Consequently, I thought, if the wall was to keep suicide bombers out, it would not really stop them; it would only make their journey more difficult.[9]

After arriving in Bethlehem we visited the Church of the Nativity and proceeded back to the bus to return to Jerusalem. As we ventured out of Bethlehem, our bus stopped in front of Bethlehem Bible College. The professor who was leading our class then grabbed the microphone and proceeded to explain that Bethlehem Bible College was an evangelical school in the heart of the West Bank. As he lauded the great work they were doing for the kingdom of God, my heart sank further. I was now approaching a full blown crisis.

Five years earlier I had stumbled into a church in Bethany. At the time I was so naïve that I never even knew that there were Christians in this land.

---

theological issues regarding land in chap. 7. For now, it must suffice to note that even if the land belongs to the Jewish people by divine right, the confiscation of land without compensation contravenes the biblical warrant. The simplest example of this is Abraham, the very one to whom the land was promised, bought land so that he might bury Sarah (Gen 23).

9. It is true that the separation barrier has coincided with the reduction of suicide bombings in Israel. It is also true that Israel has legitimate security needs and that building such a barrier is well within their rights. The barrier, however, creates numerous human rights issues. For one, though Israel has a right to build such a barrier in order to protect its citizens, they do not have the right to build it on someone else's property. Much of the barrier cuts deep into the West Bank and is not on the border that separates Israel from the Palestinian territories. The entire city of Bethlehem is well within the West Bank and not near the border with Israel. The fact that in many places the barrier butts directly up against the city of Bethlehem and the fact that the wall around Bethlehem is built entirely on Palestinian land means that it serves primarily to protect Israeli settlers. But these settlers live within Palestine (or the Palestinian territories), which is illegal by every international standard (no country is allowed to place its own citizens within the borders of a land that is not their own). If these settlers did not live in the West Bank, the wall would not be built around Bethlehem, cutting off its citizens from their own farmlands.

Now I was looking out the window of a bus in the heart of Bethlehem only to learn that not only were there Christians in this land, but that there were enough of them that they had a Bible college to train their leaders. This could only mean that some of the people in Palestine that were suffering were Christians.[10]

WHAT WAS I TO DO?

For years, I had lived within a worldview that proposed that physical/ethnic Israel was God's chosen people and that the Holy Land belonged to them in accord with the Old Testament (OT) promises. I had strongly advocated the conviction that if we blessed the physical descendants of Abraham, God would bless us; and if we cursed them, God would curse us. All of this was right in my Bible. I viewed the miraculous regathering of the nation of Israel in 1948 and 1967 as a fulfillment of prophecy. This was surely the result of the hand of God. And all of this was surely a sign that the return of Jesus was near at hand.

Suddenly, as I sat on this bus and stared out my window into the reality of the situation in Bethlehem (a situation far more complex than I was able to comprehend both then and even now), I began to question everything. For I was seeing injustice on every side. I knew deep down that in some ways I was responsible for this mess. After all, I had advocated vociferously for a political agenda of unquestioning support for the modern nation of Israel. And Israel, partly in response to injustices perpetrated against them, partly out of a desire to protect their own people just two generations removed from one of the most atrocious crimes in the history of human-ity, partly out of fear, and perhaps a whole host of factors, had taken the support of the Western powers and responded by committing injustices of their own against the people of the West Bank and Gaza.[11]

The fact that some of the Palestinian people were Christians only in-tensified my concerns. Now is this the only reason why Christians should stand up and cry out against the injustices in the Holy Land? Not at all. We

10. I realize that it is not okay that Palestinian Muslims are suffering. But you must understand that my right wing upbringing had led me to believe that all Palestinians were Muslims and that their suffering was likely the result of their terrorist convictions. This, of course, is not true. But such is the kind of naïve convictions that I was raised with and was still slowly breaking through.

11. In saying this I am not suggesting that the Palestinians are wholly innocent. They are certainly guilty of injustices also.

are called to be peacemakers. We hold to a worldview that suggests that all human beings are of supreme value. And that all human beings, Israelis and Palestinians included, have value and dignity.

The reality is that we cannot effectively fulfill the mission of God's people by unquestioningly supporting one side. The Israeli/Palestinian conflict is composed of a vast array of complex issues. The multitude of political, social, and economic issues cannot be resolved easily. But peace will not come to the people of this land, whether they be Christians—Messianic Jews or Palestinian Christians—Jews, or Muslims, if the forces of the West continue to promote the aims of one side over and against another. It is time for the church to be the conscience of the state and not its tool.[12]

12. To suggest that my story is one in which I began as pro-Israel but now have become pro-Palestine is to fail to understand my story. I certainly started with a worldview that supported one side over against another (Israel over Palestine). Now, I realize that God does not give us that option.

Part 2

A Biblical Look at the Promises of Temple, People, and Land

Over the next four chapters I intend to take a theological look at Scripture in order to examine the questions: Do the promises of family and land to Abraham and his descendants still apply today? And, if so, in what way? What I intend to accomplish in this part is to address the theological issues at the heart of the debate pertaining to Israel/Palestine. I will begin with a theological examination of the issues of temple (chap. 5), the people of God (chap. 6), and the land of promise (chap. 7).

Chapter 4

All God's Promises: Fulfilled in Jesus

Jesus answered them, "Destroy this temple, and in three days I will raise it up." The Jews then said, "It took forty-six years to build this temple, and will You raise it up in three days?" But He was speaking of the temple of His body.

—John 2:19–21

The fundamental theological assumption that undergirds my entire understanding of Scripture is that the fulfillment of all God's promises is found in Jesus.[1] I will argue that the very nature and purpose of the temple, the people of God, and the land, all point to Christ. As a result, all the promises of Scripture with regard to these are fulfilled in Christ.

The defense of this assertion is simple: it was how Jesus, Paul, and the writers of the NT understood Scripture. The basis of this affirmation is found most clearly in Paul's assertion in 2 Corinthians, "For as many as are the promises of God, in Him they are yes" (2 Cor 1:20). Taking this verse to its fullest extent means that Jesus is the fulfillment of all God's promises, including those to Abraham. The result is that Jesus is the interpretive key to unlocking the Scriptures.[2] As Paul says,

---

1. This position was argued at length in my book *Understanding Eschatology*. Readers would do well to consult this work for a more detailed understanding.

2. Hermeneutics is the "science" of interpretation. Therefore, in saying that Jesus is the interpretive key I am suggesting that all Scripture points to and through Jesus for its fulfillment. That is, any issue raised in Scripture must be viewed through the lens of the NT and Jesus. See Dalrymple, *Understanding Eschatology*, chap. 3.

> For I want you to know how great a struggle I have on your behalf and for those who are at Laodicea, and for all those who have not personally seen my face, that their hearts may be encouraged, having been knit together in love, and *attaining* to all the wealth that comes from the full assurance of understanding, *resulting* in a true knowledge of God's mystery, *that is*, Christ *Himself*, in whom are hidden all the treasures of wisdom and knowledge. (Col 2:1–3)

JESUS: THE NATURE AND PURPOSE OF TEMPLE, FAMILY, AND LAND

The merry-go-round approach to theological debating would have us simply citing an arsenal of verses that support our positions. The reason why this approach is rarely successful is because each side reads the Scriptures in light of their own set of assumptions (or hermeneutic).[3] The problem is the assumptions that the Christian Zionists adhere to and by which they read and interpret Scripture. The Zionist position assumes that a "literal" reading of the Bible is the only proper method of interpretation. My position is that a "Christological" reading *is* the proper method for interpreting the Bible. That is, the Bible is about Jesus. This does not deny a "literal" reading. In fact, I would contend that this is the "literal" reading—assuming that by "literal" one means the reading that was intended by the author(s). Whatever assumptions we take to the text are most often the very things we find in the text.

I will take a different approach to these questions. Instead of simply asserting that the promises of temple, family, and land[4] have been fulfilled by Jesus, I will contend that the very nature and purpose of these promises point to Christ. That is, they must have been fulfilled by Jesus because he represents the very essence of the promises.

In particular, I will contend in chapter 5 that the nature and purpose of the temple is such that it represents the place of God's presence on the earth. God's desire was not to simply dwell in a garden or a building (e.g., Solomon's or Herod's temple). Instead, God desired to dwell among all

3. By "hermeneutic" I mean the method of interpretation. See Dalrymple, *Understanding Eschatology*.

4. Granted that it seems odd to conclude that the land promises are fulfilled in Jesus. What will be essential here is to understand the purpose for the promise of land to Abraham. We will then see that the promise of land pointed to something greater. That something greater was accomplished by Christ.

people and throughout the entire world. I will then contend that Jesus is not only the fulfillment of the OT prophecies concerning the temple, but that he embodies in himself the fulfillment of the very nature and purpose of the temple; namely, to be the place of God's presence among his people.

This contention corresponds well with the theme of G. K. Beale's work *The Temple and the Church's Mission*. Beale states, "My thesis is that the Old Testament tabernacle and Temples were symbolically designed to point to the cosmic eschatological reality that God's tabernacling presence, formerly limited to the holy of holies, was to be extended throughout the whole earth."[5]

I will further argue that in the incarnation of Jesus the initial fulfillment of God's intention to dwell among his people has arrived. This initial fulfillment in Christ is then carried forth, through the indwelling of the Spirit, in the life of the NT people of God—for we too are temples of God! Finally, the consummation of God dwelling among his people is found in the New Jerusalem, which is the ultimate dwelling place of God.

In particular, I will argue that the two primary facets of the temple are fulfilled in Christ—namely, that the temple represents the presence of God among his people, and that God's presence was to extend throughout the entirety of the earth. We will then see that this fulfillment in Jesus is extended, by means of the Spirit, to the people of God. And that this fulfillment reaches a climax in the New Jerusalem. Understanding this is vital for discerning the manner in which the promises relating to the people of God and the land are likewise fulfilled in Jesus, the NT people of God, and the New Jerusalem.

In addition to this, it is essential to understand that one cannot completely address the issues surrounding the people of God and the land apart from the theme of the temple. This will be addressed in detail in the following chapters. At this point I will simply affirm that the temple represents the place (land) where God dwells among his people (family).

I will argue first (chap. 5) that the promise of God's temple presence has indeed begun to be fulfilled in Christ. Christ fulfills the very nature of the temple because he is the presence of God among us. As a result, he is the true temple of God. Then I will argue that the purpose of the temple is being fulfilled by the indwelling presence of the Holy Spirit in the life of the people of God today. The ultimate fulfillment of the purpose of the temple is the New Jerusalem. For, in the New Jerusalem, which I will argue is a

5. Beale, *Temple and the Church's Mission*, 25.

temple, God will dwell among all the nations (family) and throughout the entirety of the earth (land).

To repeat, Jesus not only fulfilled the OT prophecies regarding the temple, but he himself embodies the very nature and purpose of the temple. It is here that Christian Zionism fails in its assertions that the Bible requires that a physical temple must be rebuilt in Jerusalem, that the Jewish people must be restored as a nation, and that the land belongs exclusively to Jewish people.[6] Such assertions fail to account for the totality of Scripture, they have too low a view of Jesus, and they do not do justice to the NT's assertions that the nature and purpose of these promises are fulfilled in Jesus.

Another reason for beginning with the theme of the temple—even though it is only tangentially relevant to a discussion on Israel/Palestine[7]— is because in many ways it is the easiest place to start. After all, the basic assumption that Jesus is the temple is virtually undisputed. We can all agree on this.[8] What I intend to show, however, is that many Christians underestimate the significance of Jesus' fulfillment of the temple. This is evident in that many also believe that the Jewish people must build a third temple in Jerusalem before the return of Christ. But, if the prophecies regarding the rebuilding of the temple have already been fulfilled in Christ, then there is no basis for the claim that a third temple will be built in Jerusalem.

In chapters 6 and 7, I will then use the very same approach by which we determined that Jesus is the fulfillment of the temple to examine the prophecies regarding the promises of family and land to Abraham. If the promises of the temple were fulfilled by Christ, then we will have established a strong foundation from which we may equally conclude that the promise of descendants (family) and land to Abraham were also fulfilled by Christ. I will, in fact, contend that the very same assumptions by which we determined that Jesus was the temple will also confirm that the OT promises related to family and land were also fulfilled in Jesus.

It is essential to note that in the following three chapters I will use *the exact same reasoning*. In fact, the outline of each of these three chapters will be identical. The only difference is that I will substitute "family" (chap. 6)

6. Not all Christian Zionists believe that a physical temple will be rebuilt in Jerusalem.

7. It is tangentially related to the discourse of Israel/Palestine because one may be a Christian Zionist without asserting that a physical temple must be rebuilt in Jerusalem. It is, of course, central because the promises of family and land are related to God's desire to dwell among his people throughout the whole of creation.

8. Which is saying something!

and "land" (chap. 7) for "temple."[9] Consequently, the same line of argumentation by which we will determine that the fulfillment of all God's promises related to the temple are found in Jesus will also lead us to conclude that the promise related to family and land are likewise fulfilled in Jesus.

TABLE 1. OUTLINE FOR CHAPTERS 5–7

Chapter 5 Temple	Chapter 6 People	Chapter 7 Land
The Temple of God: Fulfilled in Jesus	The People of God: Fulfilled in Jesus	The Land: Fulfilled in Jesus
The Nature and Purpose of the Temple	The Nature and Purpose of the People of God	The Nature and Purpose of the Land
Provisions until the Fulfillment	Provisions until the Fulfillment	Provisions until the Fulfillment
The Fulfillment of the Temple in the NT	The Fulfillment of the People of God in the NT	The Fulfillment of the Land in the NT
Jesus as the Temple	Jesus as the People of God	Jesus as the Land
Through the Spirit the NT People of God are the fulfillment of the Temple	Through the Spirit the NT people of God are the Fulfillment of the People of God	Through the Spirit the NT People of God are the Fulfillment of the Land
The New Jerusalem Is the Consummation of the Temple of God	The New Jerusalem Is the Consummation of the People of God	The New Jerusalem is the Consummation of the Land

All in all, we will find that Jesus is the fulfillment of all God's promises to Abraham. He is the true Israel—i.e., the "beloved son" and the true people of God. The result is that for one to be part of the family of God, one must be in Jesus. Furthermore, Jesus is also the fulfillment of the land promises. And it is by being rooted in him—the true vine—that we can bring his kingdom to the whole of the earth. When read in light of Christ, the Scriptures gain a depth and a beauty that transcends the simplistic gospel that we have come to embrace. Jesus came not only to die for our sins, but to fulfill the grand story of Scripture and the wondrous plan of redemption.[10]

9. See table 1.

10. In *Understanding Eschatology: Why it Matters*, I argue that this grand story of Scripture that finds its fulfillment in Jesus also pertains to the mission of God's people. That is, we are called to be the agents through which God builds his kingdom. This has several implications as it pertains to the Israeli/Palestinian conflict. First, it means that we are called to be the light of the world. This light, however, does not shine very brightly when we advocate solely for one nation over/against another. Furthermore, as I will

Granted, for many this is a new way of understanding Scripture. I assure you that this manner of reading Scripture attempts first and foremost to put Christ at the center. It is my conviction that one cannot put too great a stress on Christ. In this, we can rest comfortably. Second, this new way of thinking is actually quite old. It is, in fact, more in line both with the historic position of the church and with the majority of scholars today.

Everything points to Jesus.

I ask readers to look carefully at what I have to say here. Prayerfully and dutifully study and consider the arguments as they are set out. I recognize that the conclusions may not fit comfortably with what many of you currently believe. But if a paradigm shift is needed, then so be it. Better to align with the Word no matter how uncomfortable one may be at first than to resist.

At the same time, if after thoughtful consideration one remains in disagreement, let us determine to move forward not as enemies but as brothers and sisters in Christ. Let us "pursue peace with all men" (Heb 12:14) and determine how we might be the peacemakers that Christ has called us to be, despite our differences.

---

contend in chap. 15, we are called as God's people to begin by caring for "the least of these brothers of Mine" (Matt 25:40). When we neglect the Christian community in the Holy Land (whether they be Israeli Christians or Palestinian Christians) we have failed in an essential duty.

Chapter 5

The Temple of God: Fulfilled in Jesus[1]

Jesus answered them, "Destroy this temple, and in three days I will raise it up." The Jews then said, "It took forty-six years to build this temple, and will You raise it up in three days?" But He was speaking of the temple of His body.

—JOHN 2:19–21

The point of the Temple . . . is that it was where heaven and earth met. It was the place where Israel's God, YHWH, had long ago promised to put his name, to make his glory present. . . . The Temple was not simply a convenient place to meet for worship. It was not even just the "single sanctuary," the one and only place where sacrifice was to be offered in worship to the one God. It was the place above all where the twin halves of the good creation intersected. When you went up to the Temple, it was not as though you were "in heaven." You were actually there.[2]

---

1. There is a significant overlap between the content of this chapter and chaps. 6–7 of my earlier book *Understanding Eschatology*. The present chapter is a somewhat condensed version of those two chapters. For a more detailed discussion the reader may consult those chapters.

2. Wright, *Paul and the Faithfulness of God*, 1:96–97.

We begin by observing the biblical notion that Jesus is the temple of God for one primary reason: it is simply the easiest place to start. After all, Christians universally agree that Jesus is the temple of God. The NT is quite clear on this. As cited above, John notes that Jesus unequivocally identifies himself as the temple (John 2:19–21). Consequently, the conclusions presented in this chapter will be readily affirmed by most all.

Many Christians, however, have not considered the significance of the claim that Jesus is the temple of God. For what does it mean to say that Jesus is the temple? And does this fact have any impact on our understanding of the OT promises that the temple would be restored?[3] The best way to answer these questions is to determine the nature and purpose of the temple. That is, what is the essence of the temple? And what is the purpose which the temple served? What I intend to affirm in this chapter is that Jesus is the fulfillment of all God's promises regarding the temple because he is the very embodiment of the nature and purpose of the temple. All the promises of God regarding the temple are fulfilled in him.

THE NATURE AND PURPOSE OF THE TEMPLE

We begin our discussion on the significance of Jesus as the temple by noting that the essential nature of the temple is that it is the place where God dwells.[4] This is seen in the description of the end-times city/temple in Ezekiel 40–48.[5] The climax of the description of this city/temple occurs in ch.

---

3. When we speak of the restoration of the temple we are presupposing the fact that the temple of Solomon was destroyed in 586 BC. The prophets who spoke after this event (including Ezekiel, Zechariah, Joel, and Haggai) indicated that God would restore, or rebuild, the temple. The question, then, becomes whether or not the restoration of the temple is something that will occur in our future or whether or not Jesus was the fulfillment of these promises. It may make some sense to suppose that the promises of the restoration of the temple must refer to a physical structure; and, consequently, must be fulfilled by a future physical temple. But, as I have been arguing here, the claims of Jesus and the NT are clear: Jesus is the temple of God. In addition, I am suggesting that the very nature and purpose of the temple is such that it must be fulfilled by the presence of God among his people in a manner that transcends a building. Thus, Jesus is God among us; and he has given us the Spirit who dwells among us. This is why, as we will see below, Paul and the NT are emphatic that the promises of the temple are fulfilled in Jesus and the life of the people of God today.

4. Cf. Ryken et al., *Dictionary of Biblical Imagery*, 849: "The temple in its most basic sense symbolizes the dwelling place of God."

5. For a complete discussion of Ezekiel's city/temple, see Beale, *Temple and the Church's Mission*.

48: "And the name of the city from *that* day *shall be*, 'The LORD is there'" (Ezek 48:35). The key element of any temple is that it is where God dwells. This is also the key feature of the New Jerusalem,[6] which is itself a city/temple, in the book of Revelation: "And I saw no temple in it, for the Lord God, the Almighty, and the Lamb, are its temple" (Rev 21:22). There is no temple in the New Jerusalem because the entire city is the place of God's dwelling! This lies at the heart of the meaning of the temple: it is the place where God dwells.

In addition to the fact that the primary feature of the temple is that it is the place where God dwells, we also see in Scripture that God's desire was not merely to dwell among his people in a building. Instead, we learn that God desires both to dwell among all people and throughout the entirety of creation.

One of the primary passages relating to the promise of God to dwell among his people is that of Leviticus 26:11–12. In Leviticus 26, the covenant promises of blessing for obedience and curses for disobedience are set forth.[7] That is, God established that if his people obeyed his laws they will be blessed and if they disobeyed his laws they will be cursed. The promise of blessings in Leviticus 26:4–13 include "rain" (26:4), "peace" (26:6), and that the people will be "fruitful and multiply" (26:9).[8] The pinnacle of these promises is found in vv. 11 and 12: "Moreover, I will make My dwelling among you, and My soul will not reject you. I will also walk among you and be your God, and you shall be My people." This list of blessings climaxes in the promise that Yahweh himself will be among them and be their God!

The importance of this passage for our understanding of the temple theme in Scripture cannot be underestimated. Its significances is confirmed by the fact that later prophetic passages referring to the promise of God's dwelling among his people cite the promise of Leviticus 26:11–12.[9]

A more careful look at the promise of God to dwell among his people in Leviticus 26:11–12 suggests that this promise is linked with the dwelling of God among Adam and Eve in the garden of Eden. Thus, in Leviticus God

6. The New Jerusalem is the eternal dwelling place of the people of God in the book of Revelation.

7. A covenant is an agreement between two parties: usually between a greater (king) and a lesser (the people). The king promises to protect and bless his subjects, while the people promise to obey the king's laws. If the people obey, they are blessed. If they disobey, they are cursed (cf. Lev 26; Deut 27–28).

8. Note the allusion to Genesis here. This will be an important point to remember.

9. Cf. Ezek 37:24–28; 2 Cor 6:14–18; and Rev 21:3–4.

promises to "walk" (Lev 26:12) among his people. This is closely linked with the dwelling of God among Adam and Eve in the garden of Eden.[10] In fact, the word "walk" (Heb: *halak*) in Leviticus 26:12 is the same as that of Genesis 3:8 where God was "walking" among Adam and Eve.[11] The connection with Genesis is also present in that the promise of blessing includes the fact that they will be "fruitful and multiply" (Lev 26:9), just as the Genesis account states (Gen 1:28).[12]

That the dwelling of God among all humanity is fundamental to the nature and purpose of the temple is evident from the description of the presence of God in the New Jerusalem. In the New Jerusalem, just as in the Garden, the presence of God will not be restricted to a building. Instead, God will dwell with humanity throughout the entirety of the New Creation (Rev 21–22). G. K. Beale concludes, "His special revelatory presence dwelt in a limited manner in human-made structures. But when he fully redeems the world and recreates it, he will fill the entire creation with his presence and dwell in it in a fuller way than ever before."[13]

This suggests that the New Jerusalem is a temple in fulfillment of the great promise of Leviticus 26 and that it also corresponds to Eden as a temple. In order to affirm that the New Jerusalem represents the fulfillment of the temple promises, we must briefly note that there is ample evidence that Eden was depicted as a garden-temple.

That Eden was understood as a garden-temple is most apparent from the fact that Eden was the place of God's presence among mankind. In addition, as with all temples, Eden was understood by the prophets to have been located on a mountain.[14] Also, the furniture of later temples was associated with Eden—for example, the lampstand in the temple was a symbol of the tree of life in the garden. In addition to this, there are numerous reasons to understand Adam and Eve as serving in Eden in accord with the roles and responsibilities of the priests in the OT sanctuary.

---

10. See Wenham, *Leviticus*, 330.

11. The verb "walk" (*mithallek*) has the exact same form in Lev 26:12 and Gen 3:8.

12. This phenomenon, whereby the description of God residing in a temple in a manner corresponding to God's dwelling among man in the Garden, is not limited to Leviticus. The famous promise to David of the construction of a temple also uses the same verb (2 Sam 7:6–7). See Collins, *Gen 1–4*, 185.

13. Beale, *Temple*, 227. Beale's work is a wonderful look at the theme of temple in Scripture. Much of the overall thrust of this chapter is indebted to Beale's work.

14. Cf. Ezek 28:14.

Eden is best understood as intended to be an earth-expanding and all-encompassing garden-temple.[15] That is, there are good reasons to believe that had Adam and Eve not sinned Eden would have expanded and the presence of God would have spread both among all mankind and throughout the entirety of the earth. This accords fully with the understanding that the temple represents the place of God's presence and that God desires to dwell among all mankind and throughout the entirety of the earth.[16]

Though some attempt to understand the promise of God's temple presence among his people in Leviticus 26:11–12 in terms of the construction of a physical temple, it is apparent that the most prominent feature of this promise in Leviticus transcends a physical building. For the essence of this promise focuses on the unhindered presence of God among his people. God promises to "walk" among them all as he did in Eden—where there were no temple buildings.[17]

PROVISIONS UNTIL THE FULFILLMENT

Early in the Genesis account Adam and Eve are expelled from the garden-temple. What was lost, in what is commonly referred to as "the fall," was far more than humankind's "innocence." Adam and Eve were expelled from God's presence! As a result, we find in the Scriptures a longing for a time when God's glorious presence would again be restored among his people. In the interim, temporary structures (namely, the tabernacle of Moses and the temple of Solomon) were erected to suffice as the temporary location of God's presence.

That these structures were temporary provisions until the fulfillment—the promised dwelling of God among his people in fullness—is evidenced by the fact that such physical buildings, by their very nature, placed

---

15. See my *Understanding Eschatology*, chap. 6; also, Beale, *Temple and the Church's Mission*.

16. See my *Understanding Eschatology*.

17. N. T. Wright affirms that the theme of Eden as a temple is also present in the book of Ezekiel: "Ezekiel's promises of a new Temple explicitly evoke the Eden theme, indicating the creator's intention to make his name known throughout the world. The eschatological promises towards the end of Isaiah link the glorious new state of Jerusalem with the promise of new heavens and new earth. Zechariah speaks of a coming huge Temple, without walls, because YHWH himself will be the wall, and 'the glory in her midst,' whereupon Israel will spread out across the world." Wright, *Paul and the Faithfulness of God*, 192.

two inherent limitations on the presence of God. For one, every physical temple building limits God's presence to one particular place. Second, such a structure also restricts the presence of God to only one person (the high priest, who alone was permitted into the holy of holies)—and even for him, only one time per year!

That the tabernacle of Moses, the temple of Solomon, or any physical structure could not have fulfilled the promise of God that he would walk among his people derives from the inherent inability of any physical structure to be the eternal dwelling place of God. This is noted by Solomon at the dedication of the temple: "Behold, heaven and the highest heaven cannot contain you, how much less this house which I have built!" (1 Kgs 8:27). This is also affirmed by the Apostle Paul, who notes that "the God who made the world and all things in it, since He is Lord of heaven and earth, does not dwell in temples made with hands" (Acts 17:24). Stephen, the first Christian martyr, similarly notes, "The Most High does not dwell in houses made by human hands" (Acts 7:48).[18] God desires to dwell among all people and throughout the whole earth. Simply put, no physical building can accomplish this.

THE FULFILLMENT OF THE TEMPLE IN THE NT[19]

Now as we look at the NT understanding of the temple we immediately are presented with the fact that the promises related to the temple and its

18. Cf. Rev 21:3–4, 22. Now this is not intended to diminish the role of the tabernacle of Moses and the temple of Solomon. They indeed sufficed temporarily as the place of God's presence among his people. They were not, however, for they could not have been, the fulfillment of God's covenant promises related to his eternal dwelling among his people. They had inherent limitations that barred them from even possibly fulfilling this role. As such, they were necessarily temporary structures. What I will now proceed to demonstrate is that after the destruction of the temple of Solomon, a number of the prophets then declared that God would restore his presence among his people. In doing so, they looked beyond the restoration of a physical structure such as the temple of Solomon, to an eternal dwelling of God in fulfillment of the purpose of the temple. These prophets, however, describe the glorious fulfillment in language befitting a glorified Eden and not a restored physical structure.

19. It is at this juncture that some have attempted to skip immediately to current events. Those who do so often contend that the OT says "x" about the temple (they usually point to the prophecies of the restoration of the temple, or they note that the major promises of the temple have not been fulfilled) and then they suggest that these promises must be fulfilled in the future (which usually means our lifetime). Hence the obsession with current events and the notion that the Jewish people are about to rebuild the temple.

restoration find their fulfillment in Jesus. This fulfillment continues, by means of the Spirit, in the life of the NT people of God. That is, as a result of the presence of the Holy Spirit in us, we too are temples. The ultimate fulfillment of the promises of God's eternal dwelling among his people occurs in the New Jerusalem.

Jesus as the Temple

That Jesus is the temple of God is fairly easy to establish and not really questioned by anyone, including Christian Zionists. What is most significant to understand, however, is that Jesus is not merely the temple in some abstract manner. Instead, he is the temple in the fullest sense and in accord with all that God has promised throughout the OT. Consequently, in the NT we find a strong affirmation that the final (or "eschatological") temple has arrived in Jesus. That is, in Jesus all of God's promises related to the temple have begun their fulfillment.[20]

This is evident in Jesus' dialogue with the Samaritan woman in John 4. Jesus informs her that the "living water" which he gives "shall become in him a well of water springing up to eternal life" (John 4:14). The term translated "well"[21] alludes to Joel 3:18, which states, "And a *spring* will go out from the house of the LORD."[22] What is significant here is that this section in Joel is a prophecy relating to the restoration of the temple.[23] This

---

The major problem with this line of reasoning is that the proponents of this thinking have skipped the NT entirely. There is not even an attempt to determine what the NT might say about the temple. Advocates of such thinking will usually concede that Jesus is the temple, but they fail to consider at all what it means to say that Jesus is the temple of God and whether or not it has any bearing on the OT promises of restoration, let alone why the NT constantly affirms that we are the temple of God. It is not at all responsible for Christians to read the OT and simply jump over the NT and proceed to the modern world. The question we must ask is how Jesus, Paul, and the NT understand the OT and the promises of the restoration of the temple.

20. I say "begun" their fulfillment because we find that the ultimate fulfillment is found in the New Jerusalem.

21. Gk *pege*.

22. The LXX (i.e., the Greek translation) of Joel 3:18 uses *pege* for "fountain." Cf. Zech 14:8.

23. When Solomon's temple was destroyed by the Babylonians in 586 BC a number of prophets, such as Joel and Ezekiel, arose and promised that God will restore the temple. These prophecies of a restored temple are some of the primary passages that Christian Zionists refer to in support of the notion that a temple will be rebuilt in Jerusalem

is evident in that chapter 3 of the book of Joel opens with, "For behold, in those days and at that time, when I restore the fortunes of Judah and Jerusalem." In addition to this, we see that the "spring" in Joel's prophecy flows from the house of the Lord, which is the temple![24] So we see that Jesus is alluding to the future restoration of God's temple as prophesied in Joel and concluding that this is what he is here to fulfill. Thus, Jesus confirms for the woman in Samaria that the promises related to the fulfillment of the temple in Joel will be experienced in him.[25]

We also see in the Gospel of Mark an understanding that Jesus is the temple of God in fulfillment of the OT promises of restoration. Mark, in fact, opens his gospel with a citation of Mal 3:1: "Behold, I send My messenger before Your face, who will prepare your way."[26] The verse in Malachi continues: "And the Lord, whom you seek, will suddenly come to His temple" (Mal 3:1b). Thus, Mark begins his gospel with a clear and emphatic declaration that John the Baptist is coming to prepare the way in fulfillment of the prophecy in Malachi. But the prophecy in Malachi refers to the coming of the Lord to his temple! And Mark sees this as fulfilled in Jesus.

Thus, Malachi prophesies a coming restoration of the temple. Mark, then, cites this verse and applies it to the announcement of the ministry of John the Baptist who prepares the way for Jesus. Thus, for Mark, Jesus is the fulfillment of the temple.

This is also evident in the closing of the gospel. Mark notes that the accusation leveled against Jesus at his trial was that he claimed, "I will destroy this Temple made with hands, and in three days I will build another made without hands" (Mark 14:58).[27] Thus, by opening his gospel with a citation from Mal 3:1, and closing it with the affirmation that Jesus is the temple, Mark has framed his gospel with references to the temple.

Interestingly, the coming of the Lord to his temple in Malachi is also in accord with the Lord returning to the land in order to bring judgment:

---

immediately prior to the return of Christ. The point I am making here is that the NT cites these passages as fulfilled in Jesus.

24. Surely the "house of the Lord" in Joel is the temple.

25. It is granted that the woman in Samaria did not understand the deeper significance of what Jesus was saying. Nonetheless, Jesus' disciples upon finding out were able to discern it—though even then not until after he had risen from the dead (cf. John 2:22).

26. Mark 1:2–3 is actually a composite citation of Mal 3:1 and Isa 40:3. Mark attributes both references to Isaiah. This is probably the result of the prominence of Isaiah.

27. That this is an allusion to the eschatological temple/kingdom of Daniel 2 will be discussed further below.

"But who can endure the day of His coming? And who can stand when He appears? For He is like a refiner's fire and like fullers' soap" (Mal 3:2). That is, the context of Malachi 3 is one of judgment.[28] And it is this theme of judgment on the temple that surrounds Mark's presentation of Jesus.[29] For Jesus' references to the Jerusalem temple in the Gospel of Mark are mostly in the negative.[30] In Mark, the temple is to be destroyed because of its lack of fruit.[31] What then will take its place? For Mark the answer is Jesus. He is the one who will build a temple not made with human hands!

The significance of this is twofold. First, we see that the prophecies of the restoration of the temple, such as in Malachi, are fulfilled in Jesus. Second, the temple that Jesus establishes is one that is not made with hands. That is, it transcends a physical building.

Through the Spirit the NT People of God are the fulfillment of the Temple

As we venture into the epistles of the NT we begin to see a transition of thought in regard to the temple. Most notably, the NT writers, beginning from the assumption that Jesus is the temple of God, then equate the NT people of God, who are themselves indwelt by the Spirit, with the temple. Jesus, though indeed the temple himself, is now viewed as the "cornerstone" of the new temple building, which itself is constitutive of the people of God: "So then you are no longer strangers and aliens, but you are fellow citizens with the saints, and are of God's household, having been built upon the foundation of the apostles and prophets, Christ Jesus himself being the cornerstone, in whom the whole building, being fitted together is growing into a holy temple in the Lord; in whom you also are being built together into a dwelling of God in the Spirit" (Eph 2:19–22).

Now, just as we earlier asked what it meant to say that Jesus is the temple, so too we ask, "What does it mean to say that the people of God

---

28. Cf. Mal 3:5.

29. Space will not allow us to explore this theme at this juncture. We note here that the fulfillment of the Lord coming to his temple (Mal 3:1; Mark 1:2) appears in Mark 11:11. Beginning at Mark 11:11 he then narrates Jesus' judgment on the temple establishment through Mark 13. See Walker, *Jesus and the Holy City*, 1–24.

30. This is because the temple establishment was commissioned to bring justice (See Mal 3:5; Jer 7:3–14) and they instead made it a den of robbers (Mark 11:17; Cf. Jer 7:11).

31. Hence the significance of the cursing of the fig tree (Mark 11:12–14, 20–25).

are the temple of God?" Is there any relationship to the prophecies of the OT regarding the restoration of the temple and the people of God being the temple of God? The answer again is unequivocally "Yes!" It is, in fact, foundational to the NT that the people of God are depicted as the temple of God in accord with the OT prophecies of the restoration of the temple.[32]

In support of this claim, we turn to 1 Corinthians to observe the manner in which Paul uses the same passage from Malachi as found in Mark. It is of great significance that Paul cites Malachi 3:2 in 1 Corinthians 3 when he informs the church in Corinth that God will judge the quality of each man's work.[33] The work to which Paul alludes is the building of God's temple![34] Paul's argument in this section of Corinthians relates to the validation of his apostleship. Paul explains that each leader in the church has been entrusted with the building of the temple of God—which is the people of God ("For we are God's fellow workers. You are God's field, God's building," 1 Cor 3:9). The foundation of this temple is none other than Christ himself: "For no man can lay a foundation other than the one which is laid, which is Jesus Christ" (1 Cor 3:11). Paul then explains that the quality of each man's work (referring to the leaders who are responsible for building the temple) will be "revealed with fire; and the fire itself will test the quality of each man's work" (1 Cor 3:13; citing Mal 3:2).

The significance of this argumentation is that Paul clearly understands that the prophecy of Malachi 3 finds its fulfillment in his present ministry. That Paul views his work as building the temple through the lives of the Corinthian Christians is confirmed by the fact that Paul concludes his argument by stating, "Do you not know that you are a temple of God, and *that the Spirit of God dwells in you?* If any man destroys the temple of God, God will destroy him, for the temple of God is holy, and that is what you are" (1 Cor 3:16–17). Paul, thus, affirms that anyone who presents himself as a leader among the people of God will be held liable for the building of God's temple—which is the church.

That the NT people of God are depicted as the temple in correlation to the promises of the OT temple is evident from the fact that Paul describes

---

32. This is summed up in Christopher Wright's observation that Paul's "argument in Ephesians 2:11–22 is saturated with Old Testament imagery." See Wright, "Christian Approach to Old Testament Prophecy," in *Jerusalem Past and Present*, 8. It is worth noting that immediately prior to his depiction of the people of God as the temple Paul cites Isa 57:19 (cf. Eph 2:17), which is a prophecy of the return of Israel from exile.

33. Cf. 1 Cor 3:13–15.

34. Cf. 1 Cor 3:8, 16.

the people of God as the temple with language that corresponds to the OT tabernacle and temple. Thus, Paul's reference to a "wise master builder" (1 Cor 3:10) alludes to the skilled workman of the tabernacle in Exodus.[35] Furthermore, Paul depicts the people of God as being constructed of "gold, silver, precious stones, wood" (1 Cor 3:12)—all items used in the construction of the temple.[36] Even more emphatically the NT affirms that God abides with us—making us by definition temples.[37]

What must be stressed is the fact that the NT not only explicitly identifies the people of God with the temple, but that it consistently does so in accord with the OT promises of restoration. This is evident in Paul's affirmation that "we are the temple of the living God" (2 Cor 6:16). In order to buttress his contention that the NT people of God are the temple of God, Paul references the OT promise: "Just as God said, 'I will dwell in them and walk among them; And I will be their God, and they shall be My people'" (2 Cor 6:16).[38] Paul's citation of the OT here is itself composed of two verses: Leviticus 26:11–12 and Ezekiel 37:26–27. As noted in the previous chapter, these two verses are central to all the prophecies relating to the future temple. They are the primary OT prophecies referring to the goal of God's dwelling among his people—Leviticus 26:11–12—and the promise of his restored presence among his people—Ezekiel 37:26–27. Paul, then, cites them as fulfilled when he applies them to the NT people of God. In the NT, then, we see that the central passages of the restoration of the temple are fulfilled by the Spirit, who is the presence of God among his people.

Finally, it is worthy of note, that we also observe, in accord with the OT prophecies of restoration, the NT people of God are presented as the temple of God in language that is appropriate to the garden of Eden. For example, Paul, in describing the NT people of God as temples in 1

35. Cf. Exod 31:4; note, this echoes Exod 35:31–32.

36. That the wood is to be included with the gold, silver, and precious stones, derives from the fact that these four items are only found together in connection with the construction of the temple (cp. 1 Kgs 5:17; 6:20–21, 28–30; also 2 Chron 3–4; cf. 1 Chron 29:2 LXX with 1 Cor 3:12)

37. Cf. 1 Cor 3:16–17; 6:19; 2 Cor 6:16; Eph 2:20–22; 1 Pet 2:5; Rev 3:12.

38. N. T. Wright notes, "*You are the temple of the living God*, he says: not to the Philippians he loved so much, not to the Thessalonians in the midst of their suffering and danger, but precisely to the recalcitrant, muddled, problem-ridden Corinthians. . . . It is simply, for Paul a fact: the living God, who had said he would put his name in the great House in Jerusalem, has put that name upon and within these little, surprised communities, dotted about the world of the north-eastern Mediterranean. Unless we are shocked by this, we have not seen the point." Wright, *Paul and the Faithfulness of God*, 1:355.

Corinthians 3:6–9, utilizes garden imagery. He introduces the people of God as garden/temples: "I planted, Apollos watered, but God was causing the growth. So then neither the one who plants nor the one who waters is anything, but God who causes the growth. Now he who plants and he who waters are one; but each will receive his own reward according to his own labor. For we are God's fellow workers; you are God's field, God's building" (1 Cor 3:6–9). This further affirms that the NT people of God are depicted in terms of the fulfillment of God's desire to dwell among his people just as he desired to do so in Eden.

The New Jerusalem Is the Consummation of the Temple of God

Finally, the promises regarding the temple, which are fulfilled in Jesus—and through the indwelling of the Spirit the NT people of God—are also applied to the New Jerusalem. The New Jerusalem provides us with the climax of God's promises to both dwell among his people and throughout the entirety of the earth.[39] This is evident from the fact that the promises of Leviticus 26:11–12 and Ezekiel 37:26–27, which are themselves central to the restoration of God's presence among his people, are also alluded to in Revelation 21 as fulfilled in the New Jerusalem.

The account of the New Jerusalem in Revelation 21–22 opens with the declaration, "And I heard a loud voice from the throne, saying, 'Behold, the tabernacle of God is among men, and He shall dwell among them, and they shall be His people, and God himself shall be among them.' . . . 'He who overcomes shall inherit these things, and I will be his God and he will be My son'" (Rev 21:3, 7). This, also, as with Paul's reference to the present dwelling of the Spirit among the NT people of God, is an allusion to Leviticus 26:11–12 and Ezekiel 37:26–27! That is, the key covenantal promises of the restoration of the presence of God among his people (Lev 26:11–12 and Ezek 37:26–27) are alluded to as fulfilled in Revelation 21:3, 7. This suggests that the New Jerusalem represents the climax of the intimacy of God among his people.

In addition to the explicit identification of the New Jerusalem with the promise of Leviticus 26 and Ezekiel 37, the entire account of Revelation 21–22 is filled with evidence that the city is indeed a temple. First, we see that John is taken to a mountain to view the holy city (Rev 21:10).

39. Cf. Rev 21–22.

The importance here is that mountains are commonly associated with temples.[40] We are also told that nothing unclean enters this city, which suggests that the entire city is sacred space.[41] Furthermore, we find that the dimensions of this city are a perfect cube in accord with the holy of holies in the OT temple[42]—suggesting that the New Jerusalem is not only a temple, which incorporates the presence of God and the Lamb, but that the entirety of the city is the holy of holies!

This corresponds well with the thesis argued above that the nature and purpose of the temple is ultimately for the presence of God to dwell among all people and throughout the entirety of the creation. For God to dwell in such a manner would indeed render the entire creation the holy of holies. This suggests that the depiction of the New Jerusalem is one in which the eschatological ("end-times") temple fills the entire cosmos of the new creation. The description of the New Jerusalem in the book of Revelation then combines temple, city, and land into one end-times picture depicting the climax of God's communion with his people.

Furthermore, it is also of great importance to note that the New Jerusalem is not depicted in correlation with the rebuilding of a physical temple like the temple of Solomon. Instead, we see that it corresponds to an Eden-like garden. The description of the New Jerusalem as an Eden-like garden is evidenced by the presence of the tree of life[43] and the river of life.[44] John notes, "And he showed me a river of the water of life, clear as crystal, coming from the throne of God and of the Lamb, in the middle of its street. And on either side of the river was the tree of life, bearing twelve kinds of fruit, yielding its fruit every month; and the leaves of the tree were for the healing of the nations" (Rev 22:1–2).

We see, then, that the prophecies of the OT restoration of the temple reach their ultimate fulfillment in the New Jerusalem. This is further supported by the fact that the narratives of the New Jerusalem and the eschatological city/temple of Ezekiel 40–48 are intricately interrelated. Both the New Jerusalem and the temple in Ezekiel 40–48 are described as cities/temples.[45] In both accounts, the prophets Ezekiel and John are taken to a

---

40. Cf. Isa 2:2–3; 66:20; Jer 26:18; 31:23; Ezek 40:2; 43:12; Mic 4:1; Ps 15:1; 24:3; 43:3.

41. Rev 21:27; 22:15; cf. 2 Chron 23:19; 29:16; 30:1–20.

42. Rev 21:16; cf. 2 Chron 3:4, 8.

43. Cp. Gen 2:9.

44. Cp. Gen 2:10.

45. Cp. "the holy city," Rev 21:10; and "like a city," Ezek 40:2.

"high mountain" to view the respective city/temples.[46] In each, the gates of the city/temple have the names of the tribes of Israel.[47] Also, the description of the respective city/temple includes a river that flows from the inner sanctum, or the throne of God himself.[48] Finally, both city/temples have trees that have leaves which are for the healing of the nations.[49]

CONCLUSION: JESUS, THE NT PEOPLE OF GOD, AND THE NEW JERUSALEM ARE THE FULFILLMENT OF THE TEMPLE

We have seen that God desires to dwell among all people and throughout the entire creation. No physical temple can therefore suffice as the eternal dwelling place of God. For all such buildings limit God's presence to one person and to one place. But, in Christ, the presence of God was no longer restricted to one person—as the Gospel of John says, "We saw His glory" (John 1:14). In the present, as a result of the Spirit's indwelling the people of God, God's presence is now experienced by more and more people. As the people of God disperse to the ends of the earth, so too God's indwelling presence transcends beyond the one place of the physical temple to the ends of the earth. Therefore, as the people of God bring forth the gospel to the ends of the earth, the presence of God extends throughout the entire earth. The presence of God among all people and throughout the entirety of the creation will climax in the New Jerusalem. Consequently, all that God has purposed in the temple is fulfilled first in the person of Christ, then in the NT people of God, and will climax in the eternal abiding of God with his people in the New Jerusalem.

46. Cf. Ezek 40:2; Rev 21:10.

47. Cf. Ezek 48:31–34; Rev 21:12–13.

48. Cf. Ezek 47:1–12; Rev 22:1–5.

49. Ezek 47:12; Rev 22:2. We could delve much further here—though space eludes us—in drawing out the connections between the prophecy of the restored temple in Ezek 36–48 and the New Jerusalem in Rev 21–22. There are numerous parallels in Ezek 36–48 to the narrative of Rev 19–22. For example, both have a summons to the birds to gorge themselves; both use "Gog and Magog"; fire comes down from Heaven and destroys Gog and his followers; both John and Ezekiel are taken to a high place where they are shown a vision of a new city; both see a figure with a measuring rod who is to measure; and the city/temple is a square with gates, walls, and foundations, and with three gates on each side; both depict God's tabernacling; both reference God's glory; both have waters flowing out of the city/temple from the throne; and both have a tree with fruit that is for healing.

Chapter 6

The People of God: Fulfilled in Jesus[1]

Now the LORD said to Abram,
"Go forth from your country,
And from your relatives
And from your father's house,
To the land which I will show you;
And I will make you a great nation,
And I will bless you,
And make your name great;
And so you shall be a blessing;
And I will bless those who bless you,
And the one who curses you I will curse.
And in you all the families of the earth will be blessed."

—GENESIS 12:1–3

But you are a chosen race, A royal priesthood, a holy nation, a people for God's own possession, so that you may proclaim the excellencies of Him who has

---

1. It is essential to note that the outlines for this chapter on the "people of God" and for chap. 7 on the "land" are identical to chap. 5 on the "temple" (see table 1). The very same line of reasoning by which we determined that Jesus is the temple of God will affirm that the fulfillment of the people of God and the land are also found in Jesus. The reader should note that the only changes in the section headings of these three chapter are that the "temple of God" (chap. 5) has been replaced by the "people of God" (chap. 6) and "land" (chap. 7).

called you out of darkness into His marvelous light; for you once were not a people, but now you are the people of God; you had not received mercy, but now you have received mercy.

—1 PETER 2:9–10

Paul's view has to do with the *fulfilment of the promises made by the creator God to Israel*, a fulfilment which is now, as the promises themselves had repeatedly indicated, not for Israel alone but for anyone at all who would heed the worldwide invitation.[2]

W ho are the people of God? For many this question is quite simple: Israel is. Others will just as readily assert that the present church is.[3] These significantly discrepant answers demonstrate the vast gulf that unfortunately has made its way into contemporary theological debates. The differences stem from our understanding of the nature of the fulfillment of the OT promises to Abraham regarding his descendants.[4] For many the promises to Abraham are straightforward and must be fulfilled exclusively by his physical/ethnic (or "literal" as some wish to contend) descendants. But, as we saw in the previous chapter with regard to the temple, the questions we ask must begin with the nature and purpose of the people of God. To simply assert that God made a promise to Abraham that must be fulfilled in some woodenly literal way by his physical descendants alone is too simple. We have already seen that the promises regarding the temple were not fulfilled in such a woodenly literal manner. Why should we assume that

---

2. Wright, *Paul and the Faithfulness of God*, 368.

3. Some even suggest that both of these positions are correct. They might postulate that Israel was and will be again the people of God, while the church currently is the people of God.

4. I fully recognize that Abraham is referred to as "Abram" until Gen 17:5, when his name is changed to "Abraham." It seems less confusing to consistently refer to him as Abraham for our purposes.

the promises regarding the family of Abraham are necessarily literal in this physical sense?

Instead, we must ask: "Why did God call Abraham?" That is, was Abraham called merely for the sake of Abraham? I will argue that an examination of the nature and purpose of God's call of Abraham confirms that the purpose of the promise of family to Abraham was that he and his descendants might be the means by which God would bless all the nations. That is, as I noted in the previous chapter, God desires to dwell among all people. And God chose Abraham to be the means through whom "all the families of the earth will be blessed" (Gen 12:3).

I will argue, then, in this chapter that just as Jesus, the NT people of God, and the New Jerusalem are the temple of God, so also, Jesus, the NT people of God, and the New Jerusalem are the fulfillment of the people of God. God's desire to dwell among all people is fulfilled in Jesus.

To affirm this we must first understand the nature and purpose of God's call to Abraham and what it means that "all the families of the earth will be blessed" through him. One of the most significant issues related to this chapter is the question of how we are to identify the people of God in the Old and New Testaments. Is there a relationship between Abraham and his descendants (i.e., "Israel"—though admittedly not all those deemed "Israel" in the OT were physical descendants of Abraham; e.g., Ruth) and the NT followers of Christ (i.e., the "church")?[5]

5. Perhaps the simplest arrangement is that found in Richard Pratt's "To the Jew First: A Reformed Perspective," chap. 9 in Bock and Glaser, *To the Jew First*. Pratt separates three distinct viewpoints among contemporary evangelicals.

First, there is the position that has become popular in the last century that sees a radical distinction between the OT Israelites and the NT church. This viewpoint, which Richard Pratt terms "Separation Theology" but is more commonly known as "Dispensationalism," understands Israel and the church as two separate peoples of God. In this line of thinking God has two distinct plans: one for ethnic Israel, and another for the NT church. Israel is conceived of as the "earthly people of God" who are to receive an earthly land in the millennium and beyond. On the other hand, the church is the "spiritual/heavenly people of God" and they will receive a heavenly inheritance. Many within this perspective contend for a strict literalistic reading of the Bible—especially when it comes to the designation "Israel." Though it varies how "literalistic" adherents of this position are, virtually all are unanimous when it comes to reading "Israel." They demand that any promises to "Israel" must be fulfilled by ethnic descendants of Abraham.

Second, there is the much-maligned view that likewise sees a radical disjunction between OT Israel and the NT church. This viewpoint, which is known as "Replacement Theology" or "Supersessionism" contends that the OT Israelites, because of their rejection of Christ, have lost their favor with God. Thus, according to this view, they have no standing before God, either now or in the future (though proponents of this view do not

As mentioned in the introduction, debates on such questions often revolve around the interpretation of this passage or that. It is my assertion that, just as we saw with the questions pertaining to the prophecies of the temple, the answers are not going to be found by arguing that "this passage" or "that" supports my definition of the people of God. Instead, we must discern the nature and purpose of the people of God. Only then can we determine how the promises to Abraham and the people of God are fulfilled. That is, once we discern why God called Abraham, then we can better discern what the fulfillment of the promises might look like.

It is essential to note that Abraham was not simply chosen for his own sake. Instead, he was chosen for a purpose. This is important. Too often, we conceive of one's being chosen in terms of the benefits that are obtained, instead of the purpose *for* which one was chosen.[6] This distinction is important. If we think of the chosen people purely in terms of a physical entity and fail to consider the purpose for which they were chosen, then we are likely to both miss the very essence of what it means to be the people of God, and fail to grasp the message of the NT concerning the identity of the people of God and their mission.

---

exclude any Jewish person from the possibility of coming to know Christ). It is important to note that the designation "Replacement Theologian" is often inappropriately placed on many theologians. The label is often used quite pejoratively and, because of this, I doubt that anyone would openly admit to holding this view.

(It is important to note that the proponents of these first two positions, who are often thought of as in radical disagreement with one another, actually have a lot in common. Most notably, they both see a significant break between the OT people of God and the NT people of God. The dispensationalist often views the promises to physical Israel as continuing into the present, with the church as a sort of interruption in God's plans. The replacement theologian views the promises to physical Israel as no longer in force because God has, as a result of their disobedience, rejected his covenant with Israel and replaced it with the church.)

Third, there is the viewpoint that suggests that the OT people of God (Israel) and the NT people of God (the church) are together the one people of God. This view, which Pratt designates "unity theology"—though I prefer the designation "fulfillment theology"—contends that there is neither separation nor replacement between the two peoples. That is, the promises to Israel in the OT are not abrogated (i.e., "put aside" or "annulled"), but fulfilled in Jesus and extended to both Jews and Gentiles as the one NT people of God. This view stresses that the people of God have always been defined as those who are chosen by God and have faith in him.

6. This is common in that many think of being chosen by God so that they can go to heaven when they die. This, though true, is not why the Scriptures say we were chosen.

THE NATURE AND PURPOSE OF THE PEOPLE OF GOD

When it comes to identifying the people of God in Scripture, as with our discussion on the temple, we begin by asking: what is the nature and purpose of the people of God? It is my contention that since all of God's promises are fulfilled in Jesus (2 Cor 1:20), we should expect to see in Jesus the fulfillment of the call of the people of God. Furthermore, in the same way that we observed that the temple of God transcends a physical building, we should not be surprised if we find that the fulfillment of the people of God also transcends the boundaries of ethnic Israel.

We begin our look at the people of God in Scripture by asking, "What was the purpose of the people of God?" To answer this we must begin in the Garden. According to the Genesis narrative, Adam and Eve were called that they might "be fruitful and multiply" (Gen 1:28), "rule" and "subdue" (Gen 1:28), "cultivate" and "keep" the garden (2:15), and live in community with one another (Gen 2:18–25). In addition, it appears that they were also to live in fellowship with God (Gen 3:8)—and this, we presume, forever. It is this intimate fellowship with God, which was the defining feature of the temple, that stood most prominently among the purposes of mankind. Furthermore, it was this fellowship with God that was lost when Adam and Eve were cursed and expelled from the garden.[7]

The expulsion of Adam and Eve made their mission much more difficult. Not only were they expelled from God's presence, but

> Cursed is the ground because of you;
> In toil you will eat of it
> All the days of your life.
> Both thorns and thistles it shall grow for you;
> And you will eat the plants of the field;
> By the sweat of your face
> You will eat bread." (Gen 3:17–19)

Thus, sin hampers humankind's efforts to fulfill our mission. In addition to all this, a new mission arose for the chosen people. For, as a result of the fall, humanity is now born in a condition in which they do not

---

7. Note that the curse and subsequent expulsion from the garden did not negate the commands to Adam and Eve to be "fruitful and multiply," nor to "rule" and "subdue" the earth, nor to "cultivate" and "keep." Instead, the curse and expulsion meant that their fulfilling these duties would be made more difficult (cf. Gen 3:17–19).

"know" God.[8] The question, then, arises: "How will God be known by the nations?"

This is the significance of the call of Abraham. Abraham and his offspring, as the new Adam, will be the means through which God rescues humanity and His creation.[9] The call of Abraham first occurs in Genesis 12:1–3:

> Now the LORD said to Abram, "Go forth from your country, And from your relatives And from your father's house, To the land which I will show you; And I will make you a great nation, And I will bless you, And make your name great; And so you shall be a blessing; And I will bless those who bless you, And the one who curses you I will curse. And in you all the families of the earth will be blessed." (Gen 12:1–3)

This call, though difficult to recognize in our English translations, contains two explicit commands: Abraham was to "go" and to "be a blessing."[10] Furthermore, we note that Abraham was not called simply for his own sake but that he might be a blessing to "all the families of the earth." Abraham and his descendants (i.e., the OT people of God) were chosen for a purpose. N. T. Wright notes, "The word 'election,' as applied to Israel, usually, carries a further connotation: not simply the divine choice *of* this people, but more specifically the divine choice of this people *for a particular purpose.*"[11] Their mission was to be the means by which God would rescue and bless all the nations. They were not called for themselves alone, but for the nations as well.

It is important to note at this juncture that, even though the people of God throughout the OT were primarily identified with an ethnicity (i.e.,

---

8. The word "know" here should connote the fullness of "knowing" God, which extends beyond the mere intellectual knowledge of God to the relational knowledge of God.

9. The relationship of Abraham and his descendants to Adam is evidenced by the consistent reiteration to be "fruitful and multiply." This command is given to Noah (Gen 9:1, 7), to Ishmael (Gen 17:20), and to Jacob (Gen 28:3; 35:11). The repetition of the divine command to Adam suggests that Abraham and the nation of Israel after him were called to fulfill the role of Adam. In fact, in the Exodus account we see that the Israelites were faithful to the commission to be "fruitful and multiply" (Exod 1:7–10). It was, in fact, their faithfulness to this mission that was the cause of Egypt's persecution of them!

10. The two commands are expressed in the Hebrew text as imperatives. As I will argue further below, these two commands are reflected in the NT by Jesus' "Great Commission" to "go" and "make disciples" (Matt 28:18–19).

11. Wright, *Paul and the Faithfulness of God,* 2:775.

the physical descendants of Abraham), this ethnic identification was not absolute. There were many who were not direct descendants of Abraham who were included into the OT people of God (e.g., Rahab, Ruth, Uriah).[12] In fact, we may assert that the limiting of the people of God to an ethnicity was neither absolute, nor intended to be permanent. Abraham was not called for the sake of himself only, but for the sake of the nations. Once the fulfillment comes, may we not conclude that the blessing of the nations continues the fulfillment of God's promises to Abraham?[13]

PROVISIONS UNTIL THE FULFILLMENT

I noted in the previous section that the goal of the temple was for God to dwell among all mankind and throughout the entirety of the earth. However, as long as the temple was restricted to a physical building the fulfillment could never come. For such a building limited God's presence to both one person and to one place. Now, in the same way that the tabernacle of Moses and the temple of Solomon were not capable of fulfilling in themselves the purpose and goal of the temple, so too we find that Abraham and the physical Israelites were not able to fulfill the role of the people of God. For the limiting of the people of God to one ethnicity could never in itself be the fulfillment of God's desire to dwell among all mankind. The call of Abraham and his descendants could not have been for them alone. Thus, as long as the people of God remained restricted to one nation the goal of

---

12. Note that both Rahab and Ruth are listed in the genealogy of Jesus (Matt 1:5).

13. This is vital to understand. After all, many will argue that the promises to Abraham were part of an everlasting covenant ("I will establish My covenant between Me and you and your descendants after you throughout their generations for an everlasting covenant," Gen 17:7). But this is precisely the point at hand. The question is not whether or not the promises were fulfilled, but the manner in which they were fulfilled. That is, if the "descendants" of Abraham in this and parallel passages are restricted to the physical offspring of Abraham, then we would have to affirm the reading that these promises must be fulfilled exclusively by those who are ethnically Jewish. But if the "descendants" of Abraham are not strictly tied to the physical descendants of Abraham, which even in the OT era they were not, then perhaps the fulfillment might be found when the "descendant" of Abraham (i.e., Jesus!) fulfills the mission of Abraham and the nations are blessed as a result. That is, when the fulfillment comes in Christ, are the nations blessed by being brought into the family of Abraham—not in replacement of Israel, but in fulfillment of Israel? If so, then it is fair to say that the promises to Abraham are still being fulfilled to this very day. There is no need to say that these promises must be fulfilled in the future by the restoration of the Jewish people. The promises have already been, and continue to be, fulfilled in Jesus and the NT people of God.

God's dwelling among all mankind would never come to fruition. We see then that Abraham was explicitly chosen for the task of being a blessing to "all the families of the earth" (Gen 12:3).

Therefore, just as the tabernacle of Moses and the temple of Solomon were temporary provisions that looked forward to the fulfillment in Christ, so also the restriction of the people of God to the choosing of Abraham and his family must be viewed in terms of a temporary provision. Abraham and his descendants were indeed set apart as the people of God. The calling of Abraham and his descendants, however, could never, in and of itself, provide the fulfillment of God's intent to dwell among all people. Instead, they were chosen as the people among whom God would dwell until the fulfillment came. Once the fulfillment came the temporary must be laid aside in order to make room for the fulfillment.[14]

As with the promises regarding the temple, so also the fulfillment of the promises pertaining to the people of God can only come through Jesus. Jesus himself is the true Adam and the perfect Israelite through whom God's call for the people of God was fulfilled.[15] As N. T. Wright concludes: "*The purpose for which the covenant God had called Israel had been accomplished, Paul believed, through Jesus.*"[16]

THE FULFILLMENT OF THE PEOPLE OF GOD IN THE NT

Now as we look at the NT understanding of the people of God we are immediately presented with the fact that the promises related to the people of God find their fulfillment in Jesus. This fulfillment, however, continues in the life and mission of the NT people of God. The ultimate fulfillment of the promises of God's eternal dwelling among all the nations occurs in the New Jerusalem.

---

14. This is the argument in Heb 7. The author of Hebrews is arguing that the Levitical priesthood served a function for a time but it was not capable of bringing in the fulfillment. Once the fulfillment came in Christ, the temporary was set aside (cf. Heb 7:11–18).

15. Now I fully recognize that this proposition is more difficult to grasp for many Western evangelicals. What I intend to show here is that this conclusion follows easily once we understand fully the extent to which all God's promises are "yes" in Christ.

16. Wright, *Paul and the Faithfulness of God*, 2:815, emphasis original.

Jesus Is the Fulfillment of the People of God

That Jesus is identified as the fulfillment of the true Israel / people of God is evident throughout the NT. First, we find that virtually every major title and attribute given to Israel is applied to Jesus in the NT. Jesus is the true Adam.[17] Jesus is the prophet of Israel who is like Moses and yet greater than Moses.[18] Jesus is the true high priest.[19] Jesus is the true king of Israel.[20] Jesus is the firstborn son of God—a title that was explicitly given to Israel.[21] And we could go on.[22]

Perhaps even more importantly, Jesus is designated as the "Son of God."[23] This title, contrary to popular opinion, does not convey the notion of Jesus' deity as much as it conveys his humanity and his identification with the people of Israel.[24] Moreover, the title "Son of God" is a title for Adam—who is deemed the "son of God" in Luke 3:38. Thus, Israel being reckoned the "son of God" was intended to display the continuity between Adam and Israel. It is in this sense that the title is used for Jesus. Consequently, Jesus is the true Adam and the fulfillment of that which Israel was called to be.[25]

Second, we see that Jesus is the fulfillment of Israel / the people of God in that he explicitly is identified as the promised "seed" of Abraham. Paul argues this in Galatians 3 when he states, "Now the promises were spoken to Abraham and to his seed. He does not say, 'And to seeds,' as *referring* to many, but *rather* to one, 'And to your seed,' that is, Christ" (Gal 3:16).[26] Consequently, "Paul's basic contention, in the area of election, was that,

17. Cf. 1 Cor 15:45.

18. Cf. Acts 3:22; Heb 3:1–6.

19. Cf. Heb 4:14.

20. Cf. Acts 2:22–36.

21. Heb 1:6; Rom 8:29; Col 1:15, 18. Note that this is emphatically true of Israel: "Then you shall say to Pharaoh, 'Thus says the LORD, Israel is My son, My firstborn'" (Exod 4:22).

22. Jesus is: Manna/Bread (John 6:32–35); Sabbath Rest (Matt 11:28; Heb 4:1–11); Sacrifice (John 1:29; Heb 10:12); Tabernacle/Temple (John 1:14; 2:19–21); Prophecy and Prophet (Matt 5:17; Heb 1:1–2); Fulfiller of the Covenant Promise (Gal 3:29); Vineyard/ Vine (John 15:1–10); Water (John 4:7–14); Light (John 8:12; 9:5); Shepherd (John 10:11). See Baker, *Two Testaments, One Bible,* 212.

23. Cf. Mark 1:1; Luke 3:38.

24. Cf. Exod 4:22; Hos 11:1.

25. Cf. Paul's argument that Jesus is the second Adam: Rom 5:12–21; 1 Cor 15:21–22.

26. Cf. Gen 22:17–18.

through the Messiah and the spirit, this God had done what he promised Abraham he would do. It's as simple as that."[27] We see, then, that Jesus is identified with the very nature of Israel / people of God.

A third means of confirming that Jesus is identified with OT Israel / people of God is that he is portrayed in accordance with the purpose of Israel. That is, we see in Jesus that the mission of the people of God is accomplished. For example, we see that in Jesus the fulfillment of Israel's call to be the witness to the nations has begun.[28] This accords with the identification of Jesus as the "faithful witness" in the book of Revelation (Rev 1:5; 3:14).[29] Also, in Luke 2:32 Simeon cites Isaiah 42:6 and 49:6 and applies them to Jesus, who is a "Light of Revelation to the Gentiles." It is, then, in accord with the role of the people of God as God's witnesses that Jesus declares himself to be "the light of the world" (John 8:12; 9:5).

Therefore, the NT writers identify Jesus as the embodiment of the nation of Israel. He is the faithful Israel who came to fulfill the very purpose for which Israel was called—namely, he came to be a light to the nations. The blessing to the nations has come in Christ. It is in light of this fulfillment that Jesus commissions his disciples and the NT people of God to "go therefore and make disciples of all the nations" (Matt 28:19).[30] The promise has been fulfilled in Christ and now it is time to bring the blessing to the nations. This commission to the nations accords with the promise to Abraham and confirms that in Christ the very purpose of the people of God has come.[31]

27. Wright, *Paul and the Faithfulness of God*, 2:784.

28. Cf. Isa 43:10 where Israel is described as God's witnesses.

29. It is quite important to the message of the book of Revelation to note that this is the very first title attributed to Jesus in the book of Revelation. See my *Revelation and the Two Witnesses*, 119–21.

30. See n30[x-ref] above connecting this commission to the promise and commission of Abraham in Gen 12:1–3.

31. At this point many within the Christian Zionist camp have come to agree that Jesus is indeed a fulfillment of God's promises to Israel / the people of God. However, they often still contend that God's promises to Israel/people must still find a "literal" fulfillment in the physical/ethnic offspring of Abraham. This suggestion fails to understand that everything Israel / the people of God were called to do was fulfilled in Jesus. There is nothing more to accomplish. The promise to Abraham and his descendants was not simply about them being something, but about them doing something. If the doing something—namely, being the means of blessing the nations—was accomplished in Jesus, and continues to be fulfilled in the mission of the NT people of God, then there is nothing left in the promises of Gen 12:1–3 to be fulfilled by some restoration of the Jewish people. Note: This does not in any way exclude the Jewish people today from being

Through the Spirit the NT People of God Are the Fulfillment of the People of God

In our look at the temple, it was noted that the fulfillment of the prophecies of the temple are found in Christ and also in the NT people of God. In the same way, when we look at the question of the nature of the people of God in the NT, we see that Jesus is identified in accordance with the people of God and in fulfillment of the role of the people of God. In addition, we also see that the NT people of God are identified both in terms of Israel and in accord with the mission of Israel. Consequently, we can assert that what God intended in the garden with Adam, for which he called Abraham and Israel (i.e., the OT people of God) to fulfill, was accomplished by Christ, and this fulfillment continues in the mission of the NT people of God.[32]

That the NT people of God are identified with Israel is first evident in that the major titles and attributes of Israel / the people of God in the OT are applied in the NT to the people of God. Peter, for example, employs numerous such titles to the people of God when he designates them as "a chosen race, a royal priesthood, a holy nation, a people for *God's* own possession" (1 Pet 2:9)—these are all titles for Israel / the people of God in the OT.[33] These titles are also paralleled in Revelation 1:6 where the people of God are described: "He has made us *to be* a kingdom, priests to His God."[34]

Likewise, Paul repeatedly depicts the people of God in terms befitting Israel / the OT people of God. Paul affirms that the NT people of God in Philippi "are the true circumcision" (Phil 3:3).[35] In Colossians, Paul refers

---

part of the covenant family of God. They are offered the same opportunity to be part of the people of God as anyone else. There is no longer "Jew nor Gentile" in the covenant people of God (Gal 3:28). Thus, through faith they too can inherit the blessings (Rom 10:8–13 "whoever believes").

32. One could easily use the word "church" here, but we must acknowledge that the church is composed of those from every nation (Jews and Gentiles), all genders, and all social classes (cf. Gal 3:28).

33. Cf. "chosen," Isa 43:20; "royal priesthood" and "holy," Exod 19:5; "people for God's own possession," Exod 19:5; Isa 43:21; Mal 3:17. Note also that 1 Pet 2:4–10 applies the same titles for Jesus and the NT people of God that are descriptive of Israel in the OT. Thus, Jesus is the "living stone" (1 Pet 2:4) and so the NT people of God are "living stones" (1 Pet 2:5), and so is Israel (Isa 28:16). Thus, Jesus is "chosen" (1 Pet 2:4) and the NT people of God are "chosen" (1 Pet 2:9), and so is Israel (Isa 43:16–20).

34. Cf. Exod 19:4–6 where Israel is likewise to be a kingdom of priests.

35. This is not replacement theology—which I will address later. Paul is affirming that through Israel, and ultimately through Jesus, the promises to Abraham and Israel are fulfilled. "In accordance with this basic Pauline conception, the polemic of Phil. 3

to the NT people of God as "those who have been chosen of God" (Col 3:12). This accords with the fact that Israel / the OT people of God are described as "My chosen people" (Isa 43:20). Furthermore, the NT people of God are deemed the "church" (Gk *ekklesia*), which throughout the Greek translation of the OT designates the gathering of Israel / the people of God.[36]

Second, we see that the NT people of God are identified with Israel / OT people of God—i.e., those who, like Abraham, believe and belong to Christ. This is seen in Paul's affirmation that Abraham is the father of "all who believe" (Rom 4:11). This is significant. Paul clearly equates the NT people of God with the descendants of Abraham. Paul further identifies the descendants of Abraham as those "who believe." In addition to this, Paul associates the early Christians with Israel / OT people of God when he affirms, "If you belong to Christ, then you are Abraham's offspring" (Gal 3:29). Paul, also, asserts, "For he is not a Jew who is one outwardly, neither is circumcision that which is outward in the flesh. But he is a Jew who is one inwardly; and circumcision is that which is of the heart, by the Spirit" (Rom 2:28–29). In the same way, Peter affirms that women are the descendants of Sarah if they do what is right: "Just as Sarah obeyed Abraham, calling him lord, and you have become her children if you do what is right without being frightened by any fear" (1 Pet 3:6).

In the NT, then, being a descendant of Abraham and Sarah is not determined by one's ethnicity, but one's faith. This redefinition of those who "believe" as the true descendants of Abraham accords with Jesus' redefinition of his family as "whoever does the will of God" (Mark 3:35; cf. 3:31–35). To claim, then, that one must be a physical Israelite in order to fulfill the promises to Abraham,[37] or that there remains two separate plans for Israel and the NT people of God (i.e., the church),[38] disregards the clear affirmation of the NT that the family of God is ultimately determined by one's faithfulness to the will of God.

Third, in addition to the fact that virtually every major title for Israel is applied to the NT people of God, we also see that the very role or purpose for Israel in the OT is applied to the NT people of God. That is, the NT

---

begins with an unequivocal assertion of the great spiritual reversal: Judaizers are the new Gentiles, while Christian believers have become the true Jews." Silva, *Philippians*, 148.

36. E.g., Deut 4:10; 9:10; 18:16; 23:2, 3, 4, 9; 31:10.

37. As the Christian Zionist does. I will address Christian Zionism more fully in chap. 9.

38. As the replacement theologian does. I will address Replacement Theology more fully in chap. 11.

people of God are depicted in terms of the very mission of Israel. Again, it must be reiterated that it is essential to understanding Scripture and the question of the people of God to recognize that Abraham and the OT people of God were called for a purpose. Many who contend that "Israel" refers only to ethnic Israel and cannot refer to the NT people of God in terms of the fulfillment often fail to consider the fact that the NT people are not simply called by the titles that belong to OT Israel, but they are also depicted in accord with this mission. It is in accord with this mission that the NT people of God are to be the "light of the world" (Matt 5:14)—a title that is applied to Israel in the OT and Jesus in the NT.[39] Interestingly, Paul applies Isaiah 42:6 and 49:6 to himself and Barnabas: "For thus the Lord has commanded us, 'I have placed You as a light for the Gentiles, that you should bring salvation to the end of the earth'" (Acts 13:47). What is significant here is to note that these very passages from Isaiah were applied by Simeon to Jesus in Luke 2:32. This point is of great significance and cannot be overlooked. Many Christians have no reservations about the fact that the role for Israel as the light of the world in Isaiah 42:6 and 49:6 is applied to Jesus in Luke 2:32. After all, Jesus is Israel / the people of God. Okay, we get that. But the question arises: "How could Paul cite the very same passage and say they were about him and Barnabas?" Are not the passages from Isaiah either fulfilled by Jesus or by Paul and Barnabas? The problem raised in this question fades away immediately once one realizes the point at hand. Namely, that Jesus is Israel / the people of God and that he accomplished the role of Israel / the people of God as the light of the world. Jesus, then, upon his death and resurrection, appointed his followers, as the renewed Israel / people of God, in order that they might continue the mission of being the light of the world. It is in this sense that Paul and Barnabas may apply Isaiah 42:6 and 49:6 to themselves. That is, even though these passages were fulfilled by Christ, Paul and Barnabas, like Jesus, were also fulfilling the mission of Israel / the people of God.

The understanding of the NT people of God as fulfilling the purpose of Israel in being a "light unto the nations" accords with the depiction of the people of God throughout the book of Revelation. From the beginning of Revelation we find that the churches are depicted as lampstands.[40] In addition, Antipas, one of the members of the church in Pergamum, is described

39. Cf. Isa 42:6; 49:6; John 8:12; 9:5.
40. Cf. Rev 1:12, 20.

as "My faithful witness" (Rev 2:13).[41] This title directly correlates with Jesus who is also declared to be the "faithful witness" (Rev 1:5). In addition, the Two Witnesses in Revelation 11 are also portrayed as faithfully performing the task as God's witnesses.[42]

Consequently, we may assert that the primary mission for Israel of being a "light to the nations" (Isa 42:6; 49:6) was fulfilled by Jesus (John 8:12; 9:5), and continues to find its fulfillment in the NT people of God (Matt 5:14). This confirms that the OT promises to Israel were for a purpose. Since Israel was called for a purpose and that purpose was accomplished by Christ and it continues to be fulfilled through the Spirit by the NT people of God, then clearly the fulfillment of the people of God has arrived.

Fourth, and perhaps most significantly, that the NT people of God are identified with Israel / the OT people of God is evident in that the great promises that God would dwell among his people (Lev 26:11–12; Ezek 37:24–28) are cited by Paul in 2 Corinthians 6:16 as fulfilled in the presence of the Spirit among the NT people of God. This is crucial for identifying the people of God in Scripture. For if God has already begun to dwell among the nations as he promised, then it stands to reason that the very purpose for choosing Abraham /Israel / the people of God is already being fulfilled. After all, the call of Abraham was so that God might bless the nations through him (Gen 12:1–3). As was noted earlier, of all the blessings listed in Leviticus 26:4–13, which were to befall on the people of God, the climax was the dwelling of God among the people. That the fulfillment of God's promise to dwell among his people has begun, according to Paul, in the NT people of God, means that the very purpose of choosing Abraham/ Israel / the OT people of God is being accomplished.[43]

---

41. My translation. The NASB reads, "My witness, My faithful one."

42. In addition to being titled "my two witnesses" (Rev 11:3), they are described as "the two lampstands" (Rev 11:4), and they are depicted as carrying out the prophetic witness of Moses and Elijah (Rev 11:5–6). See my *Revelation and the Two Witnesses* for a more complete examination of the Two Witnesses.

43. We might then ask, what purpose would even remain for the future establishment of the ethnic descendants of Israel? To claim that the Jewish people must be restored because God made promises to Abraham that can only be fulfilled by the ethnic descendants of Abraham is a failure to understand that the calling of Abraham was for a mission. Since that mission was fulfilled by Jesus, and continues to be fulfilled in the mission of the people of God today, then there remains no purpose for a further restoration of ethnic Israel.

Now this, of course, is not to suggest that the Jewish people today have no place in the will of God. After all, the purpose for the call of Abraham was to bless all nations.

The NT people of God, then, are not to be viewed as some divine interruption in which God chooses to save some from the nations until he consummates his plan for Israel.[44] Instead, God's plan for Israel, as we have seen, has been fulfilled in Christ—the one who is the true "light of the world" (John 8:12; 9:5)—and through Christ continues to be fulfilled in the NT people of God—who are also the "light of the world" (Matt 5:14).[45]

The New Jerusalem Is the Consummation of the People of God

Some may object to these conclusions on the basis of the fact that the promises to Abraham / Israel / the OT people of God do not appear to have reached a total fulfillment. After all, the restoration of Edenic conditions has not occurred. The peace and prosperity promised in the OT have not come; neither have the promises of the OT that include the complete restoration of all things, the destruction of sin and death, and the ushering in of the new creation.[46] Indeed this is true. To claim, however, that the promises are awaiting some future fulfillment exclusively by the physical descendants of Abraham fails to recognize that the promises have begun to find their fulfillment in Jesus and through the Spirit in the NT people of God.

The claim that the promised fulfillment has not arrived also fails to understand the nature of the kingdom of God. Jesus indicated that the kingdom of God would begin as a mustard seed and only after much time would it become larger than all the garden plants.[47] This indicates that

---

Surely, all nations includes the Jews. After all, "whoever" in "whoever believes will in Him have eternal life" (John 3:15) means "whoever" and certainly does not exclude the Jewish people. The inclusion of the Jewish people today into the family of God is not meant to be divorced from the people of God.

44. It has been commonplace among many dispensationalists to refer to the church age (the present time) as the "great parenthesis." This was meant to refer to the fact that in their understanding the OT was the era of Israel and the coming millennial kingdom was also the time of Israel. The intervening time was that of the church age and was merely a parenthesis between the times belonging to Israel.

45. I will stress again that this is not "Replacement Theology." The church does not replace Israel any more than Jesus replaces Israel. Jesus and the NT people of God are the fulfillment of God's promises to Abraham and Israel. To those who object and claim that the promises are only to the physical descendants of Abraham I would note here that any Jewish person can indeed receive the blessings of the covenant by means of faith in Jesus. This is not a Jew versus church issue. For many Jewish people are members of the church.

46. Isa 65:17–25.

47. Cf. Mark 4:30–32.

kingdom would start small and over time encompass the whole world. In this light, we have seen that the very purpose for which God called Abraham / Israel / the OT people of God has begun to be fulfilled in Jesus and continues in the life of the NT people of God. Thus, essential components of the fulfillment are already present—most notably the dwelling of God among us (2 Cor 6:16). It is, of course, also true that other vital components of these promises are not yet present—most notably the ushering in of universal peace (Isa 11:6–9). What shall we conclude?

It is my contention that the promise of God to dwell among his people and to restore Eden-like conditions will climax with the coming of the New Jerusalem.[48] The New Jerusalem, then, is the consummation of all God's promises related to the people of God. It is here that people from every nation and all tribes have come in fulfillment of all God's promises to Abraham. Indeed they will outnumber the stars.[49] And they will fill the whole earth.[50] It must be reiterated that the goal was not simply that Abraham would have a lot of descendants, but that "all the families of the earth will be blessed" (Gen 12:3). That is, the goal was that God might dwell in the presence of all the nations as he intended with Adam!

Central to understanding the New Jerusalem as the consummation of the fulfillment of the promises to the people of God is the fact that the New Jerusalem is equated with the people of God. Thus, though the New Jerusalem is described as a city, it is identified in terms of the people. This is evident in the description of the New Jerusalem in Revelation 21:9–10. In Revelation 21:9, John is told, "Come here, I shall show you the bride." Now, we know that the bride is the people of God (Rev 19:7–10). Thus, we are expecting that John will see the people of God. However, the next verse says that he "showed me the holy city, Jerusalem, coming down out of heaven" (Rev 21:10). So did John then see a city instead of seeing the people of God? Or shall we conclude that the bride is the city?

That John saw the city which is the bride is confirmed by John's use of "hearing" and "seeing" in the book of Revelation.[51] John uses this rhetorical device to connect two things that initially appear to be mutually exclusive.

---

48. Cf. Rev 21–22.

49. Cf. Gen 15:5; 22:17; 26:4; Rev 7:9.

50. Though the New Jerusalem is measured, it appears that it encompasses the whole earth. For the only description of the new creation in Rev 21–22 is the New Jerusalem.

51. Cf. also the hearing in Rev 7:4 with the seeing of Rev 7:9. See my "These are the Ones."

A careful investigation confirms that John wishes to identify them. For example, in Revelation 5:5–6 John hears that the "Lion" has overcome (Rev 5:5). When he turns to look, presumably to see the Lion, he sees instead a "Lamb standing, as if slain" (Rev 5:6). Now we know that in the book of Revelation Jesus is both the Lion and the Lamb. Thus, though it appears as though what John "hears" and "sees" are not the same, we soon realize that they are in fact *identical*.

In the same way, in Revelation 19 John is told (he "hears") that he will see the bride, but instead he is shown (he "sees") a city. For John, then, the city and the bride are the same. As a result, the New Jerusalem is not to be identified simply in terms of a place. The New Jerusalem depicts the gloriousness of the dwelling of the people of God in the presence of God himself.[52] Though this thought may be difficult to grasp, it is in reality no different that Jesus' identifying himself as the temple. In both instances we have an inanimate object (city/temple) being identified with people (Jesus / the NT people of God).

Furthermore, as noted in the previous chapter, the New Jerusalem is the consummate temple. Consequently, to identify it as the people of God is perfectly reasonable. For, in the same way that Christ and the people of God are described as the temple, so, also, the people of God are now depicted as a city.

That the New Jerusalem is the consummation of God's purpose for the people of God is also evident from the fact that it includes people from every nation. John's description includes: "The nations shall walk by its light" (Rev 21:24) and "they shall bring the glory and honor of the nations into it" (Rev 21:26). This corresponds well with the great multitude depicted in Revelation 7 as a group "which no one could count, from every nation and all tribes and peoples and tongues" (Rev 7:9).[53] The idea then is that at the consummation the people of God are composed of people from every nation.[54] The implication is that the New Jerusalem represents the fulfillment of God's promise to Abraham that he would be "the father of a multitude of nations."[55]

---

52. Rev 21:3, 7.

53. That the great multitude are viewed in fulfillment of the Abrahamic promises, see my "These are the Ones."

54. Cf. Rev 7:9; cf. Rev 5:9; 22:2.

55. Gen 17:4; Cf. Gen 12:3.

Further indications that the New Jerusalem must be understood in terms of the promise of God that he would dwell among all people is the fact that the great promises of Leviticus 26:11–12 and Ezekiel 37:24–28 are alluded to by John in application to the New Jerusalem in Revelation 21:3, 7!

CONCLUSION: JESUS, THE NT PEOPLE OF GOD, AND THE NEW JERUSALEM ARE THE FULFILLMENT OF THE PEOPLE OF GOD

Though one is prone to assume that the descendants of Abraham are limited to a physical nation/ethnicity, we see that the people of God were called for a mission that extended beyond an individual ethnicity. That mission was to be the means by which God would bless all nations. We find in the NT that Jesus is the "seed" of Abraham and that he is the fulfillment of the purpose and mission for Israel. That mission is then carried forward, through the Spirit, by the NT people of God—who fulfill the role of Abraham and the OT people of God. For this reason, Jesus redefines family as those who believe in him. Thus, Paul declares that Abraham is the father of all who believe. This mission will continue to be carried forth until it finds its ultimate fulfillment in the New Jerusalem, which is composed of people from all nations.[56]

The NT affirms, then, that the purpose of the people of God—to bless all the nations—has begun in Jesus, it continues—by means of the Spirit— in the life of the NT people of God today—who themselves are composed of people from many nations—and will climax in the New Jerusalem, where people from every nation enjoy the eternal presence of God among them.

---

56. Note that this paragraph is identically worded with the conclusion to the previous chapter. The only differences between them is that the terms designating the "temple" have been changed to refer to the "people of God."

Chapter 7

The Land: Fulfilled in Jesus[1]

Ask of Me, and I will surely give the nations as Your inheritance,
And the *very* ends of the earth as Your possession.

—PSALM 2:8

Now the LORD said to Abram, "Go forth from your country, and from your relatives and from your father's house, to the land which I will show you; and I will make you a great nation, and I will bless you, and make your name great; and so you shall be a blessing; and I will bless those who bless you, and the one who curses you I will curse. And in you all the families of the earth will be blessed."

—GENESIS 12:1–3

In sum, the theme of "land" is "Christified" in the New Testament.[2]

1. It is essential to note that the outlines for this chapter is also identical to the previous two chapters (see table 1). As previously noted, the very same line of reasoning by which we determined that Jesus is the temple of God will affirm that the fulfillment of the people of God and the land are also found in Jesus. The reader should be reminded that the only changes in the section headings of these three chapters are that the "temple of God" (chap. 5) has been replaced by the "people of God" (chap. 6) and "land" (chap. 7).

2. Waltke, "Kingdom of God in Biblical Theology," 22.

John deliberately presents, "the replacement of 'holy places' by the person of Jesus."[3]

The whole world is now God's Holy Land.[4]

The Jewish symbol of "the land" has been transposed by Paul (with some second-Temple Jewish antecedents) into the reality of the whole world, now claimed by the creator as the Messiah's inheritance. The ultimate Jewish symbol of space, the Temple, has been transposed by Paul, again with some antecedents, into the reality of the new community where the living God dwells in his glory, anticipating the filling of the whole world with that same glory. Thus the close relationship between the Temple and the holy land has been transposed into the close relationship between the *ekklesia* [church] and the whole world.[5]

Israel, as a corporate Adam, must spread out to subdue the earth and fill it with [God's] glory.[6]

For it is written that Abraham had two sons, one by the bondwoman and one by the free woman. But the son by the bondwoman was born according to the flesh, and the son by the free woman through the promise. This is allegorically speaking: for these *women* are two covenants, one *proceeding* from Mount Sinai bearing children who are to be slaves; she is Hagar. Now this Hagar is Mount Sinai in Arabia, and corresponds to the present Jerusalem, for she is in slavery with her children. But the Jerusalem above is free; she is our mother.

—GALATIANS 4:22–26

3. Davies, *Gospel and Land*, 334. Note: Davies is not advocating Replacement Theology. The choice of words here is somewhat unfortunate, but not meant as an affirmation of such. I will address Replacement Theology in chap. 11.

4. Wright, *Simply Christian*, 125–26.

5. Wright, *Paul and the Faithfulness of God*, 555.

6. Beale, *Temple and the Church's Mission*, 143.

When it comes to the questions of the land promises in the Scripture,[7] as with our discussions on the temple and the people of God, we must again ask, "What is the nature and purpose for the land?" Why did God grant the Holy Land to Abraham and his offspring? Far too often the assertion is made that the land in Scripture assumes a certain identity without any consideration of the nature and purpose of God's promise of land to Abraham and later to his descendants. But if, as it has been argued, all of God's promises are fulfilled in Jesus (2 Cor 1:20), then should we not expect to find that the same is true for the fulfillment of the promises of land in the NT? That is, I will assert that the promises of land are fulfilled in Jesus, continue to be fulfilled in the life of the NT people of God, and are ultimately fulfilled in the New Jerusalem.

Admittedly, the notion that Jesus, the NT people of God, and the New Jerusalem are the fulfillment of the promises of land to Abraham is a bit more difficult to grasp. This is due primarily to the fact that it is challenging to comprehend how a personal being such as Jesus, or beings such as the people of God, could fulfill the nature and purpose of a non-personal object like land. We must remind ourselves, however, that we did not have such a difficulty when we came to the conclusion that Jesus and the NT people of God are the temple of God! As such, we see that people are fulfilling the nature and purpose of an inanimate object. In addition to this, we might note that Jesus declared himself to be the fulfillment of many things that are inanimate: including "bread" (John 6:35, 41, 48, 51), "light" (John 8:12; 9:5; cf. Matt 5:14), and a "door" (John 10:7, 9). Furthermore, we might recall that the New Jerusalem represents both a place (it is the holy city; Rev 21:2, 10) and persons (it is the bride; Rev 21:9).

In addition to this, we see throughout Scripture that the city of Jerusalem is personified. This fact should not be difficult to grasp. The prophetic utterances to Jerusalem are often referring to the people and not the bricks and mortar. Jerusalem, in fact, is used for the people of God on a number of occasions.[8] For example, Jesus says, "Jerusalem, Jerusalem, who kills the prophets and stones those who are sent to her! How often I wanted to gather your children together, the way a hen gathers her chicks under her wings, and you were unwilling" (Matt 23:37). In saying this, Jesus was

---

7. The land is promised to Abraham and his descendants in Gen 12:1, 7; 13:15; 15:18; 17:8; 24:7; 26:4; 28:13; 35:12. It is reiterated throughout the OT; cf. Exod 3:8; Deut 6:3; 1 Chr 16:18; 2 Chron 20:7; Hen 9:8; Ps 105:10–11.

8. See also Isa 41:27; 49:14; 51:17.

not referring to the city but the people of the city. In Isaiah 40:2, we find that Jerusalem's sins have been forgiven. Of course, the city itself did not sin, but the residents. Such imagery, where a place is personified, is present even in the NT. In Hebrews 12:22 the author depicts the people of God as Jerusalem, "But you have come to Mount Zion and to the city of the living God, the heavenly Jerusalem, and to myriads of angels." As Peter Walker observes, "'Jerusalem' and 'Zion' can have a certain ambiguity about them. 'Jerusalem' often stands for the people themselves ([Isa] 40:2; 41:27; 49:14; 51:17)."[9] We see, then, that the application of the land and places to people is not uncommon. If, then, a city represents the people, then it is not difficult to see how the land may well find its fulfillment in Jesus and the people of God.

This chapter will examine the promises regarding the land. As with the previous chapters the argumentation will follow the exact same pattern as chapters 5 and 6 on the temple and the people. Essentially, I will argue that just as Jesus fulfills the nature and purpose of the temple and the people, so also the nature and purpose of the land finds its fulfillment in him. We will then see that the fulfillment of the land promises continue in the life of the NT people of God as they go out to all the earth. The climax of the land promises is found in the New Jerusalem—where God's presence fills all the lands.

THE NATURE AND PURPOSE OF THE LAND

As with the questions relating to the promises of the restoration of the temple and the fulfillment of the people of God, so too we must ask if the prophecies of the restoration of the land to Israel find their fulfillment in Jesus, the NT people of God, and ultimately the New Jerusalem. To answer this question we must ascertain what the nature and purpose of the land was. For if one were to simply assume that "the land" refers only to the physical geographical area that was granted to Abraham and the Israelites, then it would be easy to assume that the fulfillment must be in terms of the same geographical land.[10] We have seen however, with regard to the prom-

9. Walker, *Jerusalem Past and Present*, 35.

10. This is the assumption of Christian Zionists. They assume—remember the primary problem in these type of discussion is not how we understand a given verse but in our assumptions as to what the text may or may not say—that "land" may only mean the physical land given to Abraham. But if "temple" refers to Jesus and to the people of

ises of the restoration of the temple, that the temple itself pointed beyond a mere physical building to a greater reality—the presence of God among his people. It is my contention that the land also points to something that transcends the particular geographical land promised to Abraham. To determine this we must understand the purpose for which God gave the land to Abraham and his descendants.

It is my contention that the purpose behind the giving of land to Abraham was that it was to be the *place* from which all lands were blessed. Just as Abraham and his offspring were to be the *people* through whom God blessed all the nations, so also the land that was given to Abraham was to be the *place* from which God would bless the entire earth. Thus, God desires to dwell among all people. And he chose *Abraham and the Israelites to be the people* through whom he would do so. Additionally, he desires to dwell throughout the entire earth. And he chose *the Holy Land to be the place* from which he would bless all lands.

PROVISIONS UNTIL THE FULFILLMENT

Once Adam and Eve were expelled from the Garden it became apparent that God's intent to dwell among all mankind throughout the entire earth was frustrated. In the same way that God permitted temporary provisions with regard to the erection of the tabernacle and the later construction of the temple as the place of his presence until the fulfillment, and just as Abraham and his offspring were chosen to be the one nation through whom God would bless all the nations, so too God set apart one land in which he would dwell among his people, and in which the people of God were to flourish and spread the knowledge of God to the nations. The land of Israel / Holy Land was to be the center to which the nations flocked.[11] This land, however, was by its very nature restricted until the fulfillment should come.[12]

The restriction of God's presence to the land given to the Israelites is evident from the fact that this limited parcel of land could never in itself have fulfilled God's intent as the place of his eternal dwelling among all

---

God, then might not "land" also refer to Jesus and the people of God? We must at least consider the possibility.

11. Cf. Isa 2:1–3.

12. "The Land, like the Torah, was a temporary stage in the long purpose of the God of Abraham." Wright, "Jerusalem in the NT," in *Jerusalem Past and Present*, 67.

mankind throughout the entire earth.[13] Thus, just as a physical temple limited the presence of God to one building, so too the provision of one particular land for the people of God limited God's presence to that land.

THE FULFILLMENT OF THE LAND IN THE NT

Now as we look at the NT understanding of the land we immediately are presented with the fact that the promises related to the land find their fulfillment in Jesus. This fulfillment, however, continues in the life of the NT people of God as we go out the nations. The ultimate fulfillment of the promises of God's blessing all the earth occurs in the New Jerusalem.[14]

Jesus as the Land

In the same way that Jesus is the fulfillment of the promises regarding the temple and the people of God, he is also the fulfillment of the land promises. One evidence of this is seen in the use of vineyard imagery in application to Jesus. The vineyard is one of the primary symbols in the OT for the land of Israel.[15] Gary Burge observes, "Hosea 10.1 makes the analogy explicit: 'Israel is a luxuriant vine that yields its fruit.' The Old Testament prophets Jeremiah (2.21; 5.10; 12.11f.), Ezekiel (15.1–8; 17.1–10; 19.10–14), and Isaiah (27.2–6) all make ample use of this imagery."[16]

---

13. I will address the particular claim that the promises to Abraham were "everlasting" in chapter 13 of this book. For now it must be noted that if the thesis of this section holds true, that the land was a temporary provision given to Abraham and Israel until the fulfillment in Christ, then we can already assert that the promises of an "everlasting" possession must look forward to the fulfillment in Christ and ultimately to the New Jerusalem.

14. Though it may appear to the average reader of the NT that the issues of land and Jerusalem are not central to the NT, they are. Peter Walker notes, "Mark and Matthew were concerned about the issue of Jerusalem, Luke even more so. . . . A central theme in the Gospel [of Luke] is the 'clash of Jesus and Jerusalem.'" Walker, *Jesus and the Holy City*, 57, citing Hastings, *Prophet and Witness in Jerusalem*, 98. Many Zionists claim that the issue of land is relatively absent from the NT. Stephen M. Vantassel notes, "I do agree that the subject [land] was not a central one for the New Testament." He, then, refers to "the relative silence of the New Testament regarding the land." Vantassel, "Calvinist Considers Israel's Right to the Land," in Smith, *Jews, Modern Israel and the New Supercessionism*, 76.

15. Cf. Ps 80:8–19; Isa 5:1–7.

16. Burge, *Jesus and the Land*, 54.

When we turn to the NT we see that Jesus reinterprets this imagery. In John 15, Jesus declares that he is the vine and the NT people of God are the branches: "I am the vine, you are the branches" (John 15:5). In making this assertion, Jesus takes one of the primary symbols of the land and applies it to himself. The significance of this claim is that Jesus has now changed the source of sustenance for the people of God. No longer is it the land, but it is now Jesus. As Gary Burge puts it, "Jesus is changing the place of rootedness for Israel."[17] Peter Walker affirms,

> The common prophetic metaphor (the Land as vineyard, the people of Israel as vines) now undergoes a dramatic shift. God's vineyard, the Land of Israel, now has only one vine, Jesus. . . . And the only means of attachment to the Land is through this one vine, Jesus Christ. He offers what attachment to the Land once promised: rootedness and life and hope.[18]

We see then that the land promises are fulfilled in Jesus. Though this may seem strange, in reality the claim that the land promises are fulfilled in Jesus is simply another way of asserting that the provisions for God's people will now be Jesus and not the land. Perhaps an easier illustration of this principle is relayed in Jesus' declaration that he is the "bread of life" (John 6:35, 48, 51). Jesus is now the source of our sustenance. No longer will our survival depend on the land. Instead, we must be rooted in Jesus. As a result, the NT affirms, as I will argue below, that the people of God are no longer be tied to one land.

To insist, then, that the land promises of the OT must find their fulfillment in a future literal restoration of the nation of Israel to the physical land fails not only to understand the nature and purpose of the land but also that in the NT the people of God find their source of sustenance in Jesus.[19] The restriction of God's presence to the Holy Land was only a temporary provision made to Abraham and his descendants until the promise was fulfilled in Jesus. The restriction of God's presence to the Holy Land itself was a temporary provision that looked forward to the time when God

---

17. Burge, *Jesus and the Land*, 54.

18. Walker, *Holy City*, 190.

19. I must reiterate that the difference between the position I am advocating in this book and the Zionist relates to the understanding of Jesus. Their Jesus is too small. I do not think that most Christian Zionists intend to minimize the person and work of Jesus. Nonetheless, this is what they have done.

would bless the entire earth! This accords with the desire for God to dwell among all mankind and throughout the entire earth.

We have noted that the temple was not to be restricted forever to a physical building, but now becomes the presence of God extending to the nations and throughout all lands. We see in the NT that the people of God are no longer restricted to one nation, but now encompass many nations— and will eventually include all the nations. In addition, we find in the NT the land of promise is no longer limited to one place, but extends to the ends of the earth.

This is evident in that the promise of inheriting the land is extended in the NT to inheriting the whole earth. Jesus explicitly states: "Blessed are the gentle, for they shall inherit the earth" (Matt 5:5). It is important to observe that Jesus uses the same language as the Psalmist who promises the blessing for the humble within Israel that they would have long life in the land.[20] Jesus, then, takes a common OT theme—land—and applies it to the whole earth.

Furthermore, in Matthew's account of the rich man and Jesus we see that Jesus commands the rich man to sell all his possessions—including his land. Matthew notes, "But when the young man heard this statement, he went away grieving; for he was one who owned much property" (Matt 19:22).[21] Why would Jesus instruct this man, or anyone else for that matter, to sell his land? If, after all, land was central to the promise to Israel—and it was—then why would Jesus instruct him to sell the very thing that God had promised to those who follow him? Perhaps, the answer is that in Jesus the fulfillment has now come. No longer was one's sustenance in the land, but in Jesus!

In addition to this, we see that in the NT the early followers of Christ were also selling their land.[22] The significance of these actions is often overlooked. Their selling of land makes sense if we conclude that the first

---

20. Cf. Ps 37:11; cf. also Ps 37:3, 9, 22, 29, 34. Note that all the major English translations employ "land" in Ps 37, but they use "earth" in Matt 5:5, even though the Greek version of Ps 37 and the Greek of Matt 5:5 utilize the same word in each (*ge*). The context is the determining factor here. In the OT, the promise of God to Israel was indeed long life in the land. In the NT, however, that promise is now that they will inherit the earth. The necessity for translating *ge* as "earth" in Matt 5:5 is that it was written to Jews and Gentiles within the church. To promise Gentiles that they would be inheritors of the land of Israel would not have been viewed as much of a reward.

21. Cf. Matt 19:16–22; Mark 10:17–22; Luke 18:18–23.

22. Cf. Acts 4:34–37.

Christians had come to understand that the promises of land were fulfilled in Christ. Now realizing that Jesus is their source of sustenance and that he has called them to go to the nations, they chose to sell their land.

Finally, we see that Paul understands that the promise of land now applies to the whole earth. On two occasions Paul refers to the OT promise of land and applies it to the whole earth. The first is in Ephesians 6:1–3. Here Paul references the command for children to obey their parents: "Children, obey your parents in the Lord, for this is right" (Eph 6:1). He then cites the OT command, as found in Deuteronomy 5:16, and notes that it contains a promise: "Honor your father and mother (which is the first commandment with a promise), so that it may be well with you, and that you may live long on the earth" (Eph 6:2–3). What is important to note here is that Paul is writing to the church in Ephesus, which is not in the land of Israel. Commanding the children of Ephesian families to honor their parents that they may live long in the "land of Israel" would not have had any force or appeal to them. The promise that they would live long on the "earth" (as reflected in every major English translation) may well have appealed to them. Thus, Paul's words must be understood as promising the Ephesian church that they would inherit the earth and not simply the Holy Land.

Similarly, in Romans 4, Paul even more emphatically declares that the promise of land to Abraham and his descendants is fulfilled in Jesus and now extends to the whole earth. Paul, in referring to the promise to Abraham, notes: "For the promise to Abraham or to his descendants that he would be heir of the world was not through the Law" (Rom 4:13). What is essential to note here is that Paul cites the promise of land to Israel but he has altered it. For, instead of "land" Paul uses "world."[23] But the OT never promises Abraham that he would inherit the "world." So, how could Paul claim such? The answer is that Paul could claim such because he has come to recognize that the promises of the OT find their fulfillment in Christ and that this fulfillment transcends the initial promise of land and now extends to the world. This promise is present in the OT in seed form. The Psalmist declares, "Ask of Me, and I will surely give the nations as Thine inheritance, And the *very* ends of the earth as Thy possession" (Ps 2:8).[24] Thus, instead of inheriting just the land of Israel, God's people now inherit the whole world!

23. The Greek here is *kosmos* and not *ge*.

24. There are such hints in the OT that the promise of land will extend to the whole world. Cf. Ps 2:8; 22:27; 72:8–11; 89:25; 105:44; 111:6; Isa 9:711:1–10; 42:1–4, 6, 10–12; 49:6; 52:10, 15; 55:1–5; 60:1–16; 66:18–21.

Now some will note that after the OT people of God were sent into exile[25] the OT reiterates the promise of land. That is, God would restore them to the land. The Christian Zionists often contend that at no point in history has the complete fulfillment of this promise taken place.[26] Therefore, they reasonably conclude that such must happen in the future.

If the assertion is correct that the NT affirms that Jesus is the fulfillment of all God's promises, and if it is correct to conclude that the promises of the land looked forward to the time when the fulfillment came, and that the fulfillment of the land promises now extend to the whole earth, then it is reasonable to assert that the promises to the people of God in the NT that they will inherit the whole earth must be seen as the fulfillment of these promises. This explains why Jesus encouraged the rich man to sell his possessions and why the early Christians did just that. The promises of the restoration of the Holy Land to the descendants of Abraham has already been fulfilled in Christ.

---

25. The "exile" refers to the removing of the people of Israel from the land. The northern kingdom of Israel was sent out of the land and taken into captivity by the Assyrians in 721 BC. The southern kingdom of Judah was later conquered and sent out of the land by the Babylonians in 586 BC.

26. Many Christian Zionists will actually affirm my thesis that the promises were fulfilled in Jesus. They will, however, then contend that such promises can have multiple fulfillments. David Pawson describes this as a "characteristic of Hebrew poetry." He adds, "A prediction can be fulfilled more than once, even in a triple as well as a double realization." Pawson, *Defending Christian Zionism*, 105. In response to Pawson, I would simply note that the only instances in which prophecies are "fulfilled" more than once is when they refer to Christ, the NT people of God, and/or the New Jerusalem. That is, a prophecy may have an original referent (As with Isa 7:14 which is cited by Pawson). It may then also refer to Christ. The "second fulfillment" (Matt 1:22–23) is Christological (i.e., having to do with Christ). This makes sense in that, as I have argued here, the nature and purpose of prophecy is such that it refers ultimately to Christ. To suggest that prophecy may have multiple fulfillments and, therefore, it can be fulfilled in Christ and at the same time have a fulfillment in the modern or future state of Israel is not defensible in light of Scripture. When Jesus and the NT indicate that a prophecy is fulfilled in Christ, even in the event of a prophecy that may already have been fulfilled earlier (such as Isa 7:14; or the fact that the land promises were viewed as fulfilled even in the OT: see the discussion in chap. 13; cf. Josh 21:43–45), they do so in the context of the fact that such prophecies find their ultimate fulfillment in Christ. To suggest that such prophecies may be fulfilled in the future by a "literal" Israel then denies that they are ultimately fulfilled by Jesus. This is a serious mistake.

Through the Spirit the NT People of God Are the Fulfillment of the Land

The suggestion that the promise of land to Abraham and the OT prophecies of the restoration of the land to Israel are fulfilled by the people of God may appear strange to many. However, we have already noted that the land, and "Jerusalem" in particular, is often personified. As a result, many of the prophecies were never intended to refer to the city itself but to the inhabitants of the city.[27] That the NT affirms that God's promise of land is fulfilled in the NT people and their inheriting the earth is evident throughout the NT.

The identification of the people of God in terms of the fulfillment of the promises of land occur in several places in the NT. For one, as noted previously, we see that Revelation identifies the people with the city of the New Jerusalem. John writes, "Then one of the seven angels who had the seven bowls full of the seven last plagues came and spoke with me, saying, 'Come here, I will show you the bride, the wife of the Lamb.' And he carried me away in the Spirit to a great and high mountain, and showed me the holy city, Jerusalem, coming down out of heaven from God" (Rev 21:9–10). John is told that he is to see "the bride, the wife of the Lamb," but when he looks he sees the "holy city, Jerusalem." By means of "hearing" one thing and "seeing" another, John interprets what is heard.[28] In this instance, the bride is the city.

In addition to this, we have also already noted that the people of God are no longer called to inherit only the land promised to Abraham. They are now summoned to the ends of the earth, which will ultimately become their inheritance when the New Jerusalem descends from heaven.[29] As

---

27. This is common even in our speech today. We might well speak of a city as a place of great wickedness. In such instances it is not the place or the buildings that produce wickedness, but the people.

28. As noted previously, the most notable example of John's "hearing" and "seeing" is Rev 5:5–6, where John *hears* that the Lion of Judah has overcome, but when he turns he *sees* a Lamb that was slain. There is no doubt that the Lion and the Lamb both refer to Jesus. The point of Rev 5:5–6 is that Jesus has become the Lion by being the Lamb! For *hearing* and *seeing* See also Rev 7:4, 9; see Dalrymple, "These Are the Ones." See also Beale, *Revelation*, 1063: "John hears that he will see the Lamb's bride and then sees 'the holy city Jerusalem,' which is thus the interpretation of what he heard." See also Smalley, *Revelation*, 131.

29. In the present, the NT affirms that the people of God have an inheritance with the saints, but it is temporarily reserved in heaven: "Who has qualified us to share in

they go, however, they represent the city of Jerusalem[30] and the temple. The significance of this is that in the prophets the city of Jerusalem was the place to which all the nations would come for worship.[31] Now, however, the NT people of God take Jerusalem and the place of God's worship to the nations as they go to the ends of the earth. This is significant. For in the OT we see that the nations were to come to Jerusalem. Thus, in Isaiah it is declared: "And many peoples will come and say, 'Come, let us go up to the mountain of the LORD, to the house of the God of Jacob; that He may teach us concerning His ways and that we may walk in His paths'" (Isa 2:3). Yet, in the NT we see that the nations do not come to Jerusalem, but that Jesus sends his disciples to the nations![32] N. T. Wright observes the significance of the fact that in the NT "the redeemer does not now come *to* Zion, but *from* Zion, going out into all the world to 'gather the nations,' not by their coming to the central symbol of ancient Judaism, but by their *becoming* the central symbol."[33]

Additionally, that God's presence would be with the NT people of God as they fulfill their mission to reach the ends of the earth is indicated in Jesus' promise "I go to prepare a place for you" (John 14:2). There are several reasons to understand these words in terms of Jesus' indication to his disciples that he would establish his temple presence within them even as they went to the ends of the earth. We should note that this promise of Jesus corresponds to the fact that in Deuteronomy it is God who was to go ahead of the OT people of God in order to prepare a place for them in the promised land.[34] Thus, as Nicholas Perrin states, "Jesus is declaring that he will do exactly what Yahweh would do for Israel: prepare a *place* where

---

the inheritance of the saints in Light" (Col 1:12); and, "Blessed be the God and Father of our Lord Jesus Christ, who according to His great mercy has caused us to be born again to a living hope through the resurrection of Jesus Christ from the dead, to *obtain* an inheritance *which is* imperishable and undefiled and will not fade away, reserved in heaven for you" (1 Pet 1:3–4).

30. Cf. Heb 12:22: "But you have come to Mount Zion and to the city of the living God, the heavenly Jerusalem."

31. Cf. Isa 2:2–4.

32. Cf. Matt 28:16–20.

33. Wright, *Paul and the Faithfulness of God*, 1:358. Note that Isa 2:3 does go on to say that "the law will go forth from Zion." But this is not the same as the NT emphasis that the people of God go to the nations. For Isa 2 is clear that "all the nations will stream to it" (Isa 2:2).

34. Cf. Walker, *Jesus and the Holy City*, 186–90.

Yahweh would establish his name."[35] It is possible, then, that the place that Jesus promises to prepare for his disciples is not some heavenly disembodied existence. Instead, it is the dwelling of God among them.[36]

In addition to this we might add that the use of "place" in "I go to prepare a place" (John 14:3; Gk *topos*) corresponds to the theme of the temple and God's desire to dwell among his people. In fact, the term "place" (*topos*) was commonly used in association with the temple. This is evident by the use of "place" in Exodus 15:17: "You will bring them and plant them in the mountain of Your inheritance, the place, O LORD, which You have made for Your dwelling, the sanctuary, O Lord, which Your hands have established."[37] The language of the Exodus account exudes imagery of the temple (note that the uses of "mountain," "place," and "sanctuary" all connote the temple). Why is this important? It is important because the context of Exodus 15 suggests that Moses was referring to the promised land. In light of Jesus' use of language that parallels Exodus 15:17, we might suggest that the fulfillment of the promised land would be found in the presence of the Spirit among his disciples. That is, the *place* for which Jesus was preparing the disciples was the presence of the Spirit among them. The allusion to Exodus 15:17 correlates this *place* with the Holy Land.

We find, then, in the NT that the fulfillment of the promise of land has come. As a result, the blessing of the whole earth is to follow. Furthermore, the people of God are no longer tied to the land but to Christ. Jesus becomes the source of sustenance for his people. He will now dwell among his people even as they spread to the ends of the earth. Of course, in doing so, the very goal of God to dwell among all his people and throughout the entire earth has begun to find its fulfillment.[38] Now, if anyone wants to be his disciple, they must no longer be attached to the land, but to Jesus.

35. Perrin, *Jesus*, 54. This may also explain the significance of the foot washing in John 13, which immediately precedes the discourse of John 14. For priests who were about to enter the inner place of the temple were compelled to wash their feet (cf. Exod 30:19–21).

36. Robert Gundry affirms that the term "place" in John 14:2–3 (Gk *topos*) is often a synonym for *abode* and "easily lends itself to the thought of the believer's position in Christ." Gundry, "In My Father's House," 71.

37. The Greek version of Exod 15:17 uses *topos* here.

38. Peter Walker observes, "John's focusing 'holy space' exclusively onto Jesus in the opening chapters inevitably raises the question: what will happen when the time approaches for the 'holy space' to be removed from this world? How does one gain access to that 'place' when it has disappeared? The answer is given in the Farewell Discourse, and focuses on the Holy Spirit." Walker, *Holy City*, 192.

The result is that the people of God are no longer limited to one place. Their identity is "in Jesus" and not in the land. For the presence of God to dwell throughout the earth, it was necessary that once the Spirit was given to the people of God, the people of God were to reach to the ends of the earth.

The New Jerusalem Is the Consummation of the Land

We have seen that the promise of land points us to Christ who is himself the source of sustenance for the NT people of God. Through the Spirit, the people of God are then commissioned to extend to the nations as those who will inherit the earth. Now we will note that the New Jerusalem is the climax of the fulfillment of the land. For, the New Jerusalem represents the place of God's presence among his people throughout the entirety of the earth.

As noted earlier, the New Jerusalem represents the people of God and their dwelling in the eternal presence of God. In accord with the arguments presented here, the New Jerusalem represents the consummation of the promises of God to dwell among his people, who are themselves composed of people from every nation in accordance with the promise to Abraham, and God's promise to dwell throughout the entirety of the earth.

That the New Jerusalem encompasses the entirety of the earth, though not explicitly stated in Revelation 21–22, may well be inferred. For one, in light of the close parallels with Eden and the New Jerusalem, and the fact that Eden was intended to expand and fill the earth, it is reasonable to suppose that the New Jerusalem, in fulfillment of Eden, fills the earth. Second, in the depiction of the New Jerusalem, John says that he saw "Jerusalem coming down out of heaven from God" (Rev 21:10). The fact that nothing else is described leaves the natural assumption to be that the New Jerusalem encompasses the entire earth.[39] Finally, that the New Jerusalem

39. Some might contend that the New Jerusalem is measured as approximately 1400 miles (Gk "12,000 stadia") in length, width, and height (Cf. Rev 21:15–17) and that this would not encompass the whole earth. That the New Jerusalem likely fills the whole earth is suggested by the fact that the area of this city is the approximate size of the known Greek world at the time. In addition, it is evident that John does not intend us to see the measurements as reflecting the actual size of the city because of the symbolic use of numbers. The city is 12,000 stadia and the walls are 144 cubits (Rev 12:16–17). The use of the number 12 and its significance for the people of God cannot be missed. Note that the names of the 12 tribes are on the gates of the New Jerusalem (Rev 12:12) and the names

fills the entirety of the new earth accords well with the thesis that God's intent was to dwell among all mankind and throughout the entirety of creation. We have seen that the New Jerusalem represents the fulfillment of the conversion of the nations, where all mankind dwells with God. Now in the New Jerusalem we see that God dwells throughout the entirety of creation.

CONCLUSION: JESUS, THE NT PEOPLE OF GOD, AND THE NEW JERUSALEM ARE THE FULFILLMENT OF THE LAND

Therefore, though one is prone to assume that the land promises are limited to a physical land, we see that the land was intended to be the place from which God would bless the whole earth. We find that Jesus declares himself to be the "vine" and that the NT people of God embody Jerusalem—the city that represents the place of God's presence. For this reason, Jesus sends his disciples to the ends of the earth.

This conclusion explains a unique feature of the NT—namely, why the issue of land is essentially absent from it. After all, as Brueggemann notes, land is "a central, if not *the central theme* of biblical faith."[40] Not only was land the central issue of the OT, but it was a central issue of the Jewish world at the time of Jesus.[41] Yet, as Burge notes, Jesus "expresses no *overt* affirmation of first-century territorial theologies."[42] Why might this be? Because Jesus understands that in him the territorialness of Judaism was fulfilled. No longer was the promise of land understood as referring exclusively to the land of promise. Now, it was the whole earth. As Waltke notes, "The paradigm shift can be inferred from the fact that the term *land*, the fourth most frequent word in the OT, is never used in the NT with reference to Canaan."[43] Thus, the early Christians, seeing no more attachment to the land, sell their lands.

---

of the 12 apostles are on the 12 foundation stones (Rev 12:14). That the city is the people (see above and note the hearing and seeing of 12:9, 10) confirms that the numbers are highly symbolic. G. K. Beale concludes, "The city's measurements are not literal, nor are they nationalistic symbols of a restored temple and Jerusalem, as in Ezek 40–48. They symbolize, rather, the inclusion of the Gentiles as part of the true temple and Jerusalem." Beale, *Book of Revelation*, 1074.

40. Brueggemann, *Land*, 3.

41. See Davies, *Gospel and the Land*; and Wright, *NTPG*, 226f.

42. Burge, *Jesus and the Land*, 40.

43. Waltke, "Kingdom of God," 21.

The promise of land, then, point us to Christ who is himself the source of sustenance for the NT people of God. Through the Spirit, the people of God are then commissioned to extend to the nations as those who will inherit the earth. All of this climaxes in the New Jerusalem, which itself represents the place of God's presence among his people throughout the entirety of the earth.

Chapter 8

Conclusion: Temple, People, Land
Fulfilled in Jesus

God's desire was to dwell among all people (family) and to inhabit the entire earth (land). And it is these that God promised to bless Abraham with if he obeyed the covenant—namely, descendants[1] and land.[2] We have seen that a physical temple building had the inherent inability to fulfill the nature and purpose of the temple. This is because such a building restricted the presence of God to one place and to one person. So also the nature of both the people of God and the land presented the same limitations. For, as long as the people of God were limited to one race, the presence of God would be restricted to one people. As a result, God's intent to bless all the nations would never come to fruition. In the same way, as long as the land of promise was tied to the physical boundaries of the Holy Land, then God's presence would never fill the earth. As a result, God's desire to bless the whole earth would never be accomplished.

When we turn to the NT we see that the fulfillment of God's desires has come in Jesus. Jesus is the true people of God (family) and the source of sustenance (land). Consequently, Jesus commands his disciples to go "even to the remotest part of the earth" (Acts 1:8)—land—and "make disciples" (Matt 28:19) of "all the nations" (Luke 24:47)—family. He promises them, "I am with you always" (Matt 28:20)—temple! There it is: God's presence

1. Gen 15:5; 22:17; 26:4; 32:12.
2. Cf. Gen 15:7, 18; 17:8.

extending to the nations and throughout the earth! The fulfillment has come!

The mission of the people of God today must be understood in terms of the fulfillment of God's desire to dwell among all persons. The people of God, who are themselves temples, are chosen to be the means by which the presence of God is made known to the nations. This began with Jesus, continues through the NT people of God, and climaxes in the New Jerusalem.

With regard to the land, the goal is for the glory of God to fill the entire earth. This too finds its fulfillment as the NT people of God complete their mission to the ends of the earth. As the people of God, who are themselves temples, proclaim the gospel to the ends of the earth, the presence of God also fills the entire earth.

Thus, it is essential to understand the role of the people of God and the land in accord with the nature and purpose of the temple. God desires to dwell among all the people and throughout the entirety of his creation. To suggest that the ethnic/physical descendants of Abraham must be restored in order to fulfill prophecy fails to account for the fulfillment in the NT.

The debates, then, over identifying the people of God today (usually cast as Israel vs. the church) and whether or not the land promises to Abraham still apply to the current descendants of Abraham are misguided.

MUST PROPHECY BE FULFILLED LITERALLY?

Now some may object that the fulfillment in Jesus and in the life of God's people today does not match up to the prophecies themselves. For example, they may note that the final temple, as described by the prophets, is far more majestic than what appears to now be the case. And, it may be argued, the prophecies appear to depict a physical temple on the earth. Though I fully understand these assertions, I will simply respond here with two basic points.

First, these assertions demonstrate a fundamental misunderstanding of the significance of Christ as the temple and of the nature of the temple itself. Jesus was physically the temple on the earth. Furthermore, through the Spirit the people of God are today physically the temple of God on the earth. At some point the New Jerusalem, which is a temple, will come "down out of heaven from God" (Rev 21:10) to the earth.

Second, it is essential to understand that the nature of the fulfillment of prophecy is often more progressive. Prophecy is often fulfilled over time and in a manner that exceeds the expectation of the prophets. This may account in part why the religious leaders of Jesus' day so radically missed the coming of Christ and the inbreaking of the kingdom of God. They had conceived of the kingdom in such a manner that they were expecting some majestic arrival of God's new king who would overthrow Rome and establish God's reign. When the kingdom arrived as a baby in a manger, and later as a crucified king, the world missed him.[3]

Unfortunately, I fear that many of us may be committing a similar mistake. We also assume that the kingdom of God will come in power and great splendor. Consequently, though we have not necessarily missed the kingdom entirely, we have failed to grasp the full nature of the kingdom of God. Indeed, the kingdom of God has come in power and splendor, but the power and splendor of God is demonstrated in love and service![4] Thus, it is my contention then that the glorious climax of God's kingdom, when the New Jerusalem arrives, has already begun. But, just as Jesus brought in the kingdom and was crowned king on the cross,[5] so too the kingdom of God is built through the suffering and persevering work of God's people.[6]

To reiterate: the goal of creation is for God to dwell among all mankind and throughout the entire earth. Just as a physical temple could not be the basis for the fulfillment because it limited God's presence to one person and to one place, so too the fulfillment could not come as long as the presence of God was restricted to one race that remained within one land. Instead, the fulfillment must transcend race and land. If, as we have argued, Jesus is the key to understanding Scripture, then we see in him the fulfillment of temple, people, and land. Through Jesus we see the glory of God among us. In the NT people of God, by means of the Spirit, we see the fulfillment beginning to come to a climax: God dwelling among all people throughout the entire earth—the consummation of which is clearly the New Jerusalem.

---

3. Note Jesus' admonition: "The kingdom of God is not coming with signs to be observed" (Luke 17:10).

4. See John 13 and Jesus' washing of the disciples' feet. This is what the kingdom of God looks like. Hence, shortly after washing the disciples' feet, Jesus concludes, "By this all men will know that you are My disciples, if you have love for one another" (John 13:35).

5. The crown of thorns was certainly significant (Matt 27:29; Mark 15:17; John 19:2–5).

6. See Dalrymple, *Understanding Eschatology*, chap. 8.

Part 3

What about Israel? Responding to Christian Zionism

Chapter 9

Introduction[1]

In October 2010, the Pew Forum on Religion & Public Life conducted a survey of evangelical leaders attending the global evangelical conference in Cape Town, South Africa.

Overall, 48 percent of the evangelicals said Israel is a fulfillment of biblical prophecy about the Second Coming of Jesus, while 42 percent said it is not.

When asked where their sympathies lie, 34 percent of global evangelicals surveyed sympathized with Israel, compared with 30 percent of American evangelicals.[2]

I have advocated throughout this book that we must read Scripture in light of Jesus. I want to assure you that this view is not something new to Christianity. The view that all God's promises, including the promises to Abraham that he would be the source of blessing to the nations and the promise of land to him and his descendants, are fulfilled in Christ, the NT

---

1. I wish it to be said at the outset that I am in no way attacking or challenging the integrity or Christian character of any Christian Zionist. I fully affirm that they are brothers and sisters in Christ. We are all members of the same body! I do, however, respectfully disagree with their position. Thus, it is with a great measure of trepidation that I proceed. The last thing I wish to do is to cause greater disunity in the church. I hope that this book can be a catalyst for further discussion. And it is my fervent prayer that such discussions proceed with grace and respect.

2. Bailey, "Is Support for Israel Waning among Evangelicals?," *Religion News Service*, April 8, 2014, http://www.religionnews.com/2014/04/08/support-israel-waning-among -evangelicals.

people of God, and the New Jerusalem accords well with the historic position of the church and is in line with the majority of Christian scholars
today. Of course, I would suggest that this is because this is how we are supposed to read Scripture. Unfortunately, over the last century many within
the popular, Western Christian world have shifted away from understanding Scripture in light of Jesus.[3] As a result, the perspective presented in
this book may come across as suspect and even new to many lay readers. I
assure you that it is not.[4]

At the same time, I am confident that the perspective presented in this
book is exciting for most readers. The biblical story, when viewed through
the lens of Christ as its fulfillment, is beautiful. God's plan all along was
to bring Christ into the world in order to be the means through which
his kingdom would come. This is the essence of a love story. The eternal,
holy God of all creation entered into our mess in order to redeem us! He
loved us so much that he came to accomplish for us what we could not accomplish ourselves. What God created Adam and Eve to do, and what God
chose Abraham and his descendants to do, God himself did! Not only that,
but then we see that God has given his Spirit to his disciples and to us and
commissioned us go to the nations and make him known! Amazing! We
have a purpose as members of God's kingdom!

Nonetheless, many may still have some lingering questions. I refer to
this as the "Okay . . . but . . ." stage. This is the point in a discussion at which
a person is prepared to move forward and accept what is for them a new
position ("okay"), but remains hesitant ("but") because they are uncertain
how this new perspective is able to address certain secondary questions. In
a conversation it often looks like this: "Okay, I see what you are saying, but
what about this or that?"

This is the most difficult element of making a shift in one's thinking.
For within our old way of thinking we had answers to all sorts of questions.
We were content, or learned to be content, with most of the answers; and
the ones we were not content with we learned to ignore. Suddenly, a new
way of thinking comes along and we resist. We resist because we are uneasy.

---

3. The viewpoint of Christian Zionism is relatively new to the Christian world.
Though it has seeds in Reformation thinking (see Robert Smith, *More Desired than Our
Owne*), it has gained much traction through the writings of several popular authors over
the past century.

4. One can consult the bibliography at the end of this work to see the significant
amount of scholarly literature that widely supports the position presented in this book.

We are uneasy because we want to know what this means in terms of all the secondary questions.

At this point we have two options: we can either choose to investigate these questions in light of this new way of seeing things, or we can retreat back to our previous way of thinking—often content with ourselves for having tried the new.

The next several chapters will endeavor to address such secondary questions with regard to Christian Zionism: most notably, "What about Israel?" In particular, I will address the Christian Zionist's common assertion that the promises of family and land to Abraham in Genesis 12 and following are unconditional promises that can only be fulfilled by the physical/ethnic descendants of Abraham. That is, Christian Zionists contend that these promises of God were not dependent upon the faithfulness of Abraham and his descendants (hence, the promises are "unconditional"), and that because they were everlasting promises, they cannot be forfeited or transferred away from the ethnic descendants of Abraham. In addition, many Christian Zionists assert that in light of God's promise to bless or curse nations and people by how they treated Abraham's offspring we must support the nation of Israel at all times.

I will begin this response to Christian Zionism by first looking at two common accusations leveled by some within the Christian Zionist movement against the position presented in this book. It must be noted that not all Christian Zionists will advance these accusations. Nonetheless, because these assertions are presented in most of the popular Christian Zionist literature they really need to be addressed.

The first claim is that the position I have argued for is either anti-Semitic or that it leads to anti-Semitism.[5] Second, I will address the common accusation that my position is one of "Replacement Theology."[6] From there, I will address the theology of Christian Zionism and the claims that the promises of God in the OT to Abraham and Israel must be fulfilled by the physical/ethnic descendants of Abraham.

My position, as I have argued throughout this book thus far, affirms that the promises to Abraham and Israel, as with all the promises of God,

5. Wikipedia says Anti-Semitism "is prejudice, hatred of, or discrimination against Jews as a national, ethnic, religious or racial group." See http://en.wikipedia.org/wiki/Antisemitism. See also http://www.jewishvirtuallibrary.org/jsource/antisem.html.

6. I will define Replacement Theology more thoroughly in chap. 11. For now, I will simply note that it is a viewpoint held to by some within Christian circles that the people of God in the NT (i.e., the church) "replaces" the people of God from the OT (i.e., Israel).

were fulfilled in Jesus. My view affirms that the promises of the OT were fulfilled by Israel. After all, Jesus was a physical/ethnic descendant of Abraham! And according to the NT, the fulfillment in Christ has been extended to the nations, just as Abraham was called to do (Gen 12:3)!

Before we begin it is important to establish a basic understanding of Christian Zionism.

Chapter 10

What Is Christian Zionism?

Simply put Christian Zionism is the belief that the OT promises to Abraham and his descendants regarding land and family are to be taken *literally*.[1] By *literally* it is assumed that they can only be fulfilled by the physical/ethnic descendants of Abraham and their physical return to the Holy Land. That is, the Christian Zionist claims that since the Bible promises Abraham that his offspring will inherit the Holy Land as an everlasting possession, then such can only be fulfilled by a restoration of the physical/ethnic Jewish people to the land. With this in mind, many advocates of Christian Zionism claim that the reconstitution of the modern state of Israel in 1948 and/or 1967 was a fulfillment of such prophecies.[2]

The result is that Christian Zionism is often combined with a strong political ideology. After all, it is often supposed, that if the land belongs by divine right to the Jewish people, then Christians must support the modern state of Israel (and many are, as Christian individuals, churches, and even

---

1. What many do not realize is that the word "literally" is problematic. What does "literally" mean? It is common even In every day communication to use figures of speech, euphemisms, exaggerations, and such. I will address this issue below. For a more thorough discussion, see Poythress, *Understanding Dispensationalists*; and Dalrymple, *Understanding Eschatology*, 49–50.

2. It is quite common for Christian Zionists to believe that the regathering of the Jewish people to the Holy Land is not only a fulfillment of biblical prophecy, but that it is a prerequisite for the second coming of Christ.

whole denominations routinely send money to help Jews return to the land and even to help build settlements in the West Bank).[3]

MUST THE BIBLE BE INTERPRETED "LITERALLY" AT ALL TIMES?

Christian Zionism claims to have the upper hand on interpreting the Bible because, it is suggested, only they read the Bible in light of its *literal* meaning. This *literal* interpretation is often supposed to be in contrast to the *allegorical* approach.[4] Christian Zionists often present these views as two extremes. Since most everyone would today agree that a purely allegorical approach to interpreting the Bible is unreasonable, the Christian Zionist position appears to be confirmed as the only viable method for reading the Bible.

One of the problems here is that we must ask what is meant by *literal*. Sandra Teplinsky, a Christian Zionist, suggests, "The literal Hebraic hermeneutic [method of reading the Bible] assumes God's Word means what it says and says what it means."[5] This statement, which on the surface sounds quite reasonable, is, however, intensely problematic. For one cannot simply assert that Scripture "means what it says." After all, the question at hand is "What does Scripture say?" This is the very question we are trying to determine. Obviously, when interpreting Scripture the question is "What does this passage mean?" However, it is simplistic to assume the meaning of a passage is its literal reading. Reading a small passage this way fails to grasp the larger meaning found in the context of the entire passage. Moreover, it is even more simplistic to think that the meaning of a passage written 2500 years ago and in a different cultural context can be understood by reading it literally.

3. See Haas, "U.S. Christians Find Cause to Aid Israel," *SFGate*, July 10, 2002, http://www.sfgate.com/news/article/U-S-Christians-find-cause-to-aid-Israel-2797871.php.

4. See Teplinsky, *Why Care about Israel*, 40–41. An allegory is where figures, places, and events do not necessarily represent actualities, but they symbolize key ideas. A purely allegorical approach to the Bible, which no one today espouses, often considers it irrelevant whether or not an event actually occurred. The important matter for an allegorical approach is what the alleged event symbolizes.

5. Teplinksy, *Why Care about Israel*, 40. David Pawson says virtually the same thing (*Defending Christian Zionism*, 113).

The problem is highlighted by the fact that not even the Christian Zionist believes that everything in the Bible is literal. Christian Zionists agree that the Bible contains figures of speech, allegories,[6] hyperbole, metaphor, and a host of other elements that renders any effort to interpret everything literally impossible.[7] For instance, God is not literally a fire ("consuming fire," Deut 4:24); nor is Jesus actually a loaf of bread ("bread of life," John 6:35, 48); nor are we to actually hate our father and mother (Luke 14:26); nor will we be pillars for all eternity ("I will make him a pillar in the temple of My God," Rev 3:12). One cannot then say that interpreting the Bible is simple because it "means what it says." The question, then, is not whether one believes in the Bible literally.

What the Christian Zionist is attempting to persuade their readers to believe is that only they take the Bible seriously. But this is just plain unfair. Many people take the Bible very seriously and are quite concerned to be faithful to the Bible at all times. Just because they do not hold to the Christian Zionist conclusions does not mean that they have adopted liberal standards that undermine the integrity of the Bible.

Furthermore, we must note that the Bible never states that everything in it must be interpreted literally. This is an important point. Most Christian Zionists affirm a view that the Bible is our authority in all matters. Yet Christian Zionism has taken a non-biblical assumption and imposed it on the Bible.

Their position must then be forced upon the Bible by some outside standard. The problem is that applying this standard to the Bible does not even make sense. After all, we do not use this standard in any other medium of communication. Our everyday speech is riddled with figures of speech, metaphors, idioms, etc. Even our written communications (newspapers, magazines, web pages, etc.) are not bound by the assumption of some strict literalism. Therefore, if we do not normally assume that all communication must be understood with a strict literalism, then why should we assume that the Bible must?

In addition to this, we must recognize that the Bible contains poetry, parables, prophetic pronouncements, and other genres that regularly

---

6. Paul refers to his illustration in Gal 4:22–31 as an allegory. So we know the Bible has at least one allegory.

7. Even Teplinsky acknowledges, "The Bible is interspersed beautifully with vivid symbolism and genuine allegory" (41).

transcend *normal* speech. All of this causes us to seriously question the assumption that the Bible must be interpreted *literally* at all times.

I recognize that this raises a serious question for many—namely, "if I do not take everything in the Bible literally, then how do I know what is literal and what is not?" Though this present book is not an attempt to answer this question fully, allow me to give a few brief comments. First, we must acknowledge that determining what the Scriptures mean is not too difficult. The reality is that the Scriptures, as with any piece of literature, must be interpreted in accord with their contexts. To determine the context we must consider a number of factors including the language, historical context, theology, culture, and customs. Certainly, in some aspects this is inherently difficult because the text was written two thousand years ago in a different historical, cultural, and linguistic context. Nonetheless, there are some parts of the biblical text that are relatively straightforward, while other parts may be more elusive.

Second, and perhaps most importantly for our present discussion, we must also understand the genre, or style of writing. That is, we must ask if the statement occurs in a poetic, historical, epistolary, or an apocalyptic context. Of course, it is important that we understand the nature of the genre at the time of writing and not as it is understood by the contemporary world. That is, we must be careful not to assume that the rules for writing and reading history, or poetry, etc., in the ancient world were necessarily the same as in our modern world.

The failure to recognize the various genres within Scripture is one of the most significant weaknesses of Christian Zionism. For example, it is too often assumed that when a prophet refers to "Jerusalem" the prophet must be referring to the literal city of Jerusalem. Yet we have many instances in Scripture in which references to Jerusalem are not to the city but the inhabitants.[8] This is true in common speech also. We may refer to a city as "such a friendly place."

Third, I would note here that we must also understand that the Scriptures are primarily about Jesus. That is, we can safely assume that the Scripture presents us with a story that climaxes with Jesus! Therefore, when we see a prophecy about the restoration of the temple, we should not be too

---

8. For example, in Matt 23:37, Jesus says, "Jerusalem, Jerusalem, who kills the prophets and stones those who are sent to her! How often I wanted to gather your children together, the way a hen gathers her chicks under her wings, and you were unwilling."

surprised to learn that the fulfillment is found in Jesus, who is truly God among us.

With this in mind, we turn now to address some of the common assertions of Christian Zionism.

MUST THE PROMISES TO ABRAHAM BE FULFILLED BY PHYSICAL/ETHNIC ISRAELITES?

It is commonplace among Christian Zionists to assert that the promises to Abraham and his descendants must be fulfilled by the physical/ethnic descendants of Abraham. Some Christian Zionists prefer to say that these promises must be fulfilled by "literal" Israel. As we have seen, however, this language is highly problematic. The question we must ask in such an instance is: what does "Israel" mean? Why should we assume, as the Christian Zionist would like us to, that it can only refer to the physical descendants of Abraham?

As we look at this question more deeply, we notice that the meaning of "Israel" was not absolute even in the OT itself. Ruth, for example, was not a direct descendant of Abraham (she was descended from Lot); yet she is listed in the genealogy of Jesus in Matthew 1:5. May we not then conclude that she was an "Israelite"? In addition, we see that Paul argues that Abraham is the "father of all who believe" (Rom 4:11). This raises the question then as to which definition of "Israel" we are to employ when looking at a prophetic statement.

For example, in Ezekiel 37:15–28, the prophet says,

> The word of the LORD came again to me saying, "And you, son of man, take for yourself one stick and write on it, 'For Judah and for the sons of Israel, his companions'; then take another stick and write on it, 'For Joseph, the stick of Ephraim and all the house of Israel, his companions.' Then join them for yourself one to another into one stick, that they may become one in your hand. . . . Say to them, 'Thus says the Lord GOD, Behold, I will take the sons of Israel from among the nations where they have gone, and I will gather them from every side and bring them into their own land; and I will make them one nation in the land, on the mountains of Israel; and one king will be king for all of them; and they will no longer be two nations and no longer be divided into two kingdoms. . . . I will deliver them from all their dwelling places in which they have sinned, and will cleanse them. And they will

be My people, and I will be their God. My servant David will be king over them, and they will all have one shepherd; and they will walk in My ordinances and keep My statutes and observe them. They will live on the land that I gave to Jacob My servant, in which your fathers lived; and they will live on it, they, and their sons and their sons' sons, forever; and David My servant will be their prince forever. I will make a covenant of peace with them; it will be an everlasting covenant with them. And I will place them and multiply them, and will set My sanctuary in their midst forever. My dwelling place also will be with them; and I will be their God, and they will be My people. And the nations will know that I am the LORD who sanctifies Israel, when My sanctuary is in their midst forever."'

The Christian Zionist assumes that this prophecy is about physical/ ethnic Israel. They then suppose that since nothing in the Old or New Testaments indicates that Ezekiel's promises were fulfilled by the physical/ ethnic descendants of Abraham, then it must refer to a future restoration of physical/ethnic Israel to the land—which some will then suggest was fulfilled in 1948 and/or 1967. Now, granted all of this makes great sense. It has as an advantage the fact that it is straightforward and simple. The meaning is clear. But is this the best way of understanding Scripture?

I have argued at length in this book that the suggestion that the promises to Abraham and the OT people of God must be fulfilled by physical/ ethnic Israel in the present or the future is greatly at odds with Scripture. We have seen that the OT promises of temple, family, and land were never intended to be restricted to a physical temple building, a particular race, or a particular land. The Christian Zionist claim that these OT promises still apply to the physical/ethnic descendants of Abraham gravely misreads the Scripture because it fails to recognize that the fulfillment has already begun in Jesus. When applying this understanding to the passage cited above in Ezekiel we see that Jesus is the "servant" who "will be king over them" (Ezek 37:24). Since Jesus is the temple of God who is with us forever, then we may conclude that when, in Ezekiel, God says that he "will set My sanctuary in their midst forever. My dwelling place also will be with them" (Ezek 37:26–27), that this too was fulfilled by Christ.

In addition, we see that Paul, in 2 Corinthians 6:16, cites Ezekiel 37:27 and applies it to the Christian community in Corinth. Furthermore, Revelation 21:3 alludes to Ezekiel 37:27 and portrays the consummation of this prophecy as occurring in the New Jerusalem.

Jesus is the fulfillment of all God's promises to Abraham. The failure to understand this basic point of Scripture is a fundamental error of Christian Zionism. Jesus was and is the consummate Israel. He is the "firstborn" son of God (Col 1:15, 18; Heb 1:6; Rev 1:5; cf. Exod 4:22). Jesus is the "light of the world" (John 8:12; 9:5; cf. Isa 42:6; 49:6). As we have seen, all that Israel was called to do and to be Jesus was and did.

THE RELATIONSHIP BETWEEN THE OT AND THE NT

Another common assertion at this point by Christian Zionists is that the NT cannot affect the meaning of the OT prophecies. In saying this, the Christian Zionist demands that we read the OT and determine its meaning without considering the NT.

The problem here is that the NT explicitly states that Jesus came to "fulfill" the OT (Matt 5:17). In addition, when we read the NT we learn that the OT was all along pointing to something greater, something deeper, and something so profound that the OT prophets themselves did not fully comprehend what they were saying. Thus, Peter affirms,

> As to this salvation, the prophets who prophesied of the grace that *would come* to you made careful searches and inquiries, seeking to know what person or time the Spirit of Christ within them was indicating as He predicted the sufferings of Christ and the glories to follow. It was revealed to them that they were not serving themselves, but you, in these things which now have been announced to you through those who preached the gospel to you by the Holy Spirit sent from heaven— things into which angels long to look. (1 Pet 1:10–12)

According to Peter the message of the prophets "predicted the sufferings of Christ" and that they were not fully grasped by the prophets, but "have been announced to you." The assertion, then, that the NT cannot affect our understanding of the meaning of the OT is incredulous.

Now, I am not saying that the NT changes the meaning of the OT. I am instead saying that the OT all along was pointing us to Christ. The OT finds the fullness of its meaning in Christ.

In saying this, I am not denying that we read the OT in light of its immediate context. Of course, we do. What I am suggesting is that in light of the coming of Christ, the NT affirms that it completes the meaning of the OT. That is, the OT only gains the fullness of its meaning when understood in light of Christ and the NT! As Karen Jobes notes, "The knowledge imparted by forewitness to the prophets is now being realized in the life of Jesus. Therefore, Peter views the gospel of Jesus Christ as one with the message of the OT."[9]

To say, then, that the NT cannot legitimately affect our interpretation of the OT is to deny that the OT points us to Jesus. Jesus, himself, declares that all of the Scriptures were about him:

> And He said to them, "O foolish men and slow of heart to believe in all that the prophets have spoken! Was it not necessary for the Christ to suffer these things and to enter into His glory?" Then beginning with Moses and with all the prophets, He explained to them the things concerning Himself in all the Scriptures. (Luke 24:25–27)

Reading the Bible in light of Jesus is what Paul means when he says,

> For as many as are the promises of God, in Him they are yes. (2 Cor 1:20)

To reiterate, this is not to say that the meaning of the OT is changed by the NT. Instead, it is enhanced by the NT. It is like a sailor looking through binoculars at a very distant land. He has a glimpse of what lies ahead. He may journal and write some basic facts about what he sees. However, he has no means of knowing precisely what native plants and animals inhabit the land. He may not even know if it is inhabited by people or civilizations. Once upon the land, the sailor may explore the land and learn all there is to know about it. Now he writes with a deep and intimate understanding of the land he once only knew from a distance.

To read the OT as though the NT did not exist is to deny the very essence of the Scriptures—namely, that the Scriptures are about Jesus. One cannot completely understand the OT without the NT. For the NT is that which the OT was pointing to all along. Nor can one fully understand the NT without seeing its relationship to the OT.

One of the most common assertions made by Christian Zionists against the position presented in this book is that my position represents "Replacement Theology." Though I recognize that most readers of this book may not be aware of Replacement Theology, it is important to address this issue here.

---

9. Jobes, *1 Peter*, 98.

What is Replacement Theology? Good question.[10] Simply understood, Replacement Theology proposes that because physical/ethnic Israel did not fulfill its calling, God chose to "replace" Israel with the church.[11]

Another way of saying it is that Replacement Theology represents one perspective in regard to the question "What is the proper way of understanding the relationship between Israel (the OT people of God) and the Church (the NT people of God)?" The Replacement Theologian answers this question by asserting that there is no relationship between the two. Israel has been rejected and *replaced* by the church.

10. I am somewhat grieved by the fact that almost everyone who uses this term has no real understanding of what Replacement Theology even means. Often those who accuse others of espousing Replacement Theology do not even attempt to define Replacement Theology or to address the arguments. Instead, the person who opposes the Christian Zionist is simply dismissed because they supposedly represent "Replacement Theology." Whatever Replacement Theology means, it must be bad, because it is almost always used slanderously.

11. H. Wayne House notes, "Essentially the view claims that the church has replaced national Israel as the recipient of the blessings of God and that the church has fulfilled the terms of the covenants given to Israel, which they rejected" ("Church's Appropriation of Israel's Blessings," in House, *Israel the Land and the People*, 78).

Chapter 11

Is This View Replacement Theology?[1]

This question warrants a simple response: No, I do not espouse Replacement Theology.

In fact, I would suggest that Replacement Theology also represents a fundamental misreading of the Bible. The NT is clearly written to show that the story of the OT and the people of God not only continues in Jesus and the NT, but that it finds its fulfillment in Jesus and the NT. I would affirm that it is foundational to the Scriptures and the character of God that God has been faithful to his promises.[2]

Ironically, it is the Christian Zionist who has more in common with Replacement Theology than my position. To explain how this is so, an understanding of the relationship between OT Israel and the NT people of God is worthy of further development. This will enable us to properly understand Christian Zionism, Replacement Theology, and the fulfillment in Christ view that I am presenting.

One of the difficulties in understanding the relationship between Israel and the church stems from the fact that many of those who advocate

---

1. Note: I am first going to give a simple answer to this question and then in the following section I will provide a more in-depth argument. For many, the simple answer should suffice. Those who want to think more deeply can entrench themselves as we will briefly venture into the philosophical realm to highlight further problems with both Zionism and Replacement Theology.

2. This is the heart of the message of Romans (and most of the NT for that matter).

Christian Zionism make it appear as though there are only two views.[3] They suggest that either one believes that "Israel" always refers to the physical, ethnic Israel—the Christian Zionist position—or that one believes that the nation of Israel has been *replaced* by the church of the NT. This is commonly presented as though one either believes in Israel as a *literal* entity, or one believes that "Israel" has been replaced by the *spiritual* Israel, which is the church. Christian Zionist Paul Benware says this explicitly: "The issue is how God will fulfill them [the prophecies regarding Abraham]—literally to Israel or spiritually to the church."[4]

Dividing this discussion into the *literal* camp versus the *spiritual* camp is intended to bias the reader. Many Christian Zionist authors commonly label any opposing viewpoint as *spiritual, allegorical,* or *symbolic.*[5] When cast in this light it is usually pretty easy for most Christians to side with the Christian Zionist position. For the Christian Zionist position has the alleged advantages of: (1) reading the Bible in a straightforward (*literal*) manner; and (2) not *spiritualizing* the Bible.

There is, however, a third position, which I have presented throughout this book. This view contends that Jesus and the NT people of God (the church) are the fulfillment of all of God's promises in the OT. Israel did not fail, because Jesus is the true Israel. Jesus' faithfulness means that God has

---

3. This is even the case in Michael Vlach's *Has the Church Replaced Israel?* Vlach uses the designation "Supersessionism" instead of "Replacement Theology." He does, however, list a variety of views of Supersessionism (see chap. 1 of his work *Has the Church Replaced Israel?*). Nonetheless, he still presents as though there are only two views: Supersessionism and Christian Zionism (though he does not use the latter title).

4. Benware, *Understanding End Times Prophecy*, 38.

5. I will address further below the problem with asserting that one is "literal/physical" and the other is "symbolic/spiritual." At this time I will simply note that the Bible and the biblical world did not think in such dualistic categories. Dividing the world between the purely "literal/physical" and the purely "symbolic/spiritual" would have made no sense to Jesus, Paul, or even Moses. Thus, the modern attempt to do so is the result of adopting a worldview that is more at home in the Enlightenment and post-Enlightenment world, than it is in the biblical world.

Even more importantly, the view that I have presented throughout this book is that the fulfillment of God's promises is in accord with both the "literal/physical" and the "symbolic/spiritual." For Jesus is "literally" the "physical" temple of God and at the same time through the Spirit the fulfillment of the temple in Jesus is "symbolic/spiritual" in that it transcends the "literal/physical" and thus God's presence dwells beyond the limits of a physical building. Therefore, the criticism of Christian Zionists of the "symbolic/spiritual" viewpoints, which they often label "Replacement Theology" or "Supersessionism," does not address the viewpoint that I have presented. In fact, as will be evidenced in this chapter, I will join in some of the criticism of Replacement Theology.

accomplished his purpose for Israel through Jesus. The blessings are now to be carried out in fullness to the nations.

A DEEPER LOOK

My simple response to the charge of "Replacement Theology" warrants clarification. First, I would affirm that God has not replaced Israel with Jesus or the church. God's promises are indeed fulfilled by Israel, or—shall I say—the descendants of Abraham. As I have already demonstrated, the Scriptures are clear that the descendant of Abraham through whom the promises are fulfilled is Jesus!

Thus, I would affirm that indeed God's promises to Israel are fulfilled by Israel. The problem here is in the understanding of who "Israel" is. We have seen that the definition of "Israel" solely in terms of the physical/ethnic race of the Jewish people does not stand up to the OT, let alone the NT. The Replacement Theologians make the same mistake as the Christian Zionist when they view the people of God in the OT exclusively as an ethnicity.

In addition, Replacement Theologians mistakenly assert that since ethnic Israel did not fulfill its role as the people of God, God has turned to the church as a replacement for Israel. But Israel did fulfill its purpose! Jesus is the true Israel and he was faithful. Replacement Theology misses the mark at precisely this point. Though Replacement Theology properly recognizes Jesus and the NT people of God as the new Israel, it fails by not recognizing that Jesus and the NT people of God are such in continuity with and in the fulfillment of the OT. The new twelve (the apostles) are the fulfillment of the old twelve (the twelve tribes). That is why in Scripture the foundation of the church is built upon the twelve apostles,[6] while the wall and gates of the city/temple have the names of the twelve tribes.[7]

Additionally, it is clear from the NT that the NT people of God (the church) are to be viewed in continuity with the OT people of God (physical/ethnic Israel). Paul affirms that the people of God are determined by those who have "the faith of our father Abraham" (Rom 4:12). He adds that Abraham is "the father of all who believe" (Rom 4:11). This is why Jesus claims that his brothers and sisters (i.e., the true Israelites) are those who do "the will of God" (Mark 3:35). Replacement Theology fails, then, because

---

6. Cf. Eph 2:20; Rev 21:14.
7. Cf. Rev 21:12–13.

it does not understand that Jesus and the NT people of God are a direct fulfillment of the OT promises.

Unfortunately, the Christian Zionist fails to recognize that the promises to Abraham were never intended to be reserved for only one ethnicity. Paul claims in Romans 4:

> For if those who are of the Law are heirs, faith is made void and the promise is nullified; for the Law brings about wrath, but where there is no law, there also is no violation. For this reason *it is* by faith, in order that *it may be* in accordance with grace, so that the promise will be guaranteed to all the descendants, not only to those who are of the Law, but also to those who are of the faith of Abraham, who is the father of us all." (Rom 4:14–16)

To suggest, as the Christian Zionist does, that there remains a future hope for the Jewish people that is distinct from the nations is essentially to affirm that this hope is distinct from Christ.[8] Equally problematic, however, is the position of Replacement Theology. For the essence of Paul's argument in Romans is that God has not abandoned his promises to Israel, but that in Jesus they have been fulfilled. As N. T. Wright affirms, "Israel had not been abandoned. It had not been 'replaced.' It had been transformed."[9]

The fundamental error, then, for both the Christian Zionist and the Replacement Theologian is the failure to understand Christ as the fulfillment of God's promises to Abraham regarding land and family. The Christian Zionist fails to understand Christ as the fulfillment. As I have already noted at length, these promises were never intended to be limited to just the ethnic descendants of Abraham alone, nor to the Holy Land only. The Replacement Theologian fails to understand that Jesus fulfilled these promises as the true Israel. The NT people of God do not replace Israel, in this sense they *are* Israel.

It is actually quite ironic then that the Christian Zionist accuses those with whom they disagree with adhering to Replacement Theology. After all, Christian Zionism has much more in common with Replacement Theology than it does with any other viewpoint. For both the Christian Zionist and the Replacement Theologian look at the Scriptures and see a radical disjunction between the OT and the NT. The Christian Zionist claims that the promises to Israel were not fulfilled by Jesus and, thus, they are still valid for ethnic Israel. For the Christian Zionist the break comes in that

8. Cf. Eph 2:12.

9. Wright, *How God Became King*, 197.

the NT era is an interruption (sometimes called the "great parenthesis") in God's plan for Israel. The Replacement Theologian similarly sees a break between the OT and the NT. For they view the promises of the OT as no longer valid for Israel because OT Israel has been replaced by the church.

My position has been that the promises to Israel are valid in the NT. They find their fulfillment, however, in Jesus (who was Jewish and Israel *par excellence*). Through Jesus the promises of God continue to find their fulfillment in the NT people of God—who are composed of Jews and Gentiles in fulfillment of God's promises to Abraham that he would bless all nations. Since Jesus is the consummate seed of Abraham, the promises have been fulfilled in him, and they continue, through the Spirit, to be fulfilled in the redeeming of the nations (which includes Jewish people).

CONCLUSION

The similarities between Christian Zionism and Replacement Theology are the result of a fundamental philosophical error. In particular, both Replacement Theology and Christian Zionism have been negatively influenced by Enlightenment thinking (which has unfortunately influenced much of popular Christian thinking).[10] One of the defining characteristics of Enlightenment thought is that it came to view everything in terms of a radical distinction between the physical world and the spiritual world.[11] It is within this dualistic manner of thinking that both the Christian Zionist and the Replacement Theologian have read the Bible as though Israel and the church are two separate entities—one physical and one spiritual.[12] That is, both see a radical break between the OT and the NT as well as between Israel and the church.

The difference between the two views is that the Christian Zionist, as a result of the assumption that the Bible is to be read literally as much as possible, assumes that God's promises to Israel of family and land must be fulfilled literally by physical Israel. The Replacement Theologian, on the other hand, assumes that Israel failed its mission and God has both rejected ethnic Israel and turned to the church to fulfill his promises.

10. In particular, I am referring to the revival of Neo-Platonism. Wright proposes that this is a revival of Epicureanism. See Wright, *Surprised by Scripture*.

11. In Neo-Platonism, the spiritual world is said to be good, while the physical world is evil.

12. They do not agree, of course, on who is the true Israel. See below.

Both views are inadequate. The Bible does not permit such a radical break between the physical and the spiritual. After all, Jesus is the temple of God—literally and spiritually.

Chapter 12

Were the Promises to Abraham Conditional or Unconditional?

Now the LORD said to Abram,
"Go forth from your country,
And from your relatives
And from your father's house,
To the land which I will show you;
And I will make you a great nation,
And I will bless you,
And make your name great;
And so you shall be a blessing;
And I will bless those who bless you,
And the one who curses you I will curse.
And in you all the families of the earth will be blessed."

—GENESIS 12:1–3

I will give to you and to your descendants after you, the land of your sojournings, all the land of Canaan, for an everlasting possession; and I will be their God.

—GENESIS 17:8

No leaving, no blessing. . . . Bluntly put, if Abraham had not got up and left for Canaan, the story would have ended right there. . . . The Bible would be a very thin book indeed.[1]

In Genesis 17:8 God promises to Abraham that he would give him and his descendants the land as "an everlasting possession." The Christian Zionist asserts that the promise was unconditional—that is, it did not depend on Abraham and his descendants' faithfulness. The Replacement Theologian, however, contends that the promise was conditional—that is, it was dependent upon Israel's faithfulness. The Replacement Theologian then contends that Israel's subsequent disobedience meant that God rejected Israel and the promise of land was null and void.

It is my intent in this chapter to address the question: "Was the promise of land to Abraham and his offspring an unconditional promise?" That is, was the promise to Abraham such that God has granted the land to Abraham and his offspring regardless of their faithfulness? The answer, which of course is never simple, is both yes and no! That is, both the Christian Zionist and the Replacement Theologian are right and they are wrong.

THE NATURE OF COVENANT PROMISES

As we attempt to unravel a very messy topic it is first important to understand that there are two questions to answer, both of which are pertinent to the present discussion. First, we must ask if the promise of land to Abraham can only be fulfilled by the physical/ethnic descendants of Abraham? Second, was the promise to Abraham conditional or unconditional? That is, was the promise of land to Abraham and his descendants dependent on their continued obedience (as argued by the Replacement Theologian), or were the promises such that since God made it, then he will do what he promised regardless of the people's faithfulness or unfaithfulness (as argued by the Christian Zionist)?

1. C. Wright, *Mission*, 206.

Must the Physical Descendants of Abraham Return to the Land?

The first question we must address is: must the OT promises of land to Abraham and his descendants be fulfilled by the physical descendants of Abraham? This question has essentially been addressed throughout this book. The seed of Abraham is Jesus. Paul emphatically declares this in Galatians 3:16: "Now the promises were spoken to Abraham and to his seed. He does not say, 'And to seeds,' as *referring* to many, but *rather* to one, 'And to your seed,' that is, Christ."

The Christian Zionist's claims that the promise of land still awaits a fulfillment by ethnic Israel fails both to account for Jesus as the clear fulfillment of God's promise, and to recognize the nature and purpose of God's choosing Abraham and his offspring and giving them the land. The land was intended to be the place from which God would bless all the earth. As noted in chapter 5 on the temple, God desires to have his eternal presence dwell among all people and throughout the whole earth. That fulfillment has begun in Jesus. The commission, therefore, now is for the people of God to go to the ends of the earth and bring the blessing of God's presence to all people and throughout the whole earth.

What does this mean for the promise of land? I will expand on the implications of this for the land as we proceed through this chapter. For now, I will note that this means that the land promises are fulfilled in Christ. The result is that the blessings have gone to all the earth.

Consequently, it is somewhat of a moot point as to whether or not the promises to Abraham were conditional or unconditional. The question would only be relevant if the promises were not fulfilled. But the promises have been fulfilled in Christ, who was the true Israelite.

The Replacement Theologians are mistaken, then, when they assert that the promises were taken from Israel because of their disobedience and given to the church (in "replacement" of Israel). They were not taken from Israel. They were fulfilled by Jesus.

The Christian Zionists are equally mistaken when they assert that the promises are unconditional and are awaiting a fulfillment in the ethnic descendants of Abraham. For they have already been fulfilled in Jesus, who was the faithful ethnic descendant of Abraham.

Are the Promises and Covenants Unconditional or Conditional?[2]

What about the Christian Zionist's contention that the promises to Abraham were not dependent upon the faithfulness of Abraham or his descendants? They argue that since "God never reneges on a promise,"[3] he must restore the descendants of Abraham to the land in fulfillment of the promise. Christian Zionist David Pawson states emphatically, "This covenant is full of 'I will' promises (count them in Genesis 12–17), but there are no 'you shall' or 'you shall not' commandments given with them. It is an unconditional offer without demands."[4] Barry Horner refers to the promises in terms of the "abiding nature of the unconditional Abrahamic covenant."[5]

Opponents of the Christian Zionist position, including those who advocate Replacement Theology, will often respond that God's promises are indeed conditional—i.e., contingent on the faithfulness of Abraham and the people. They contend that God may well rescind a promise of blessing if the people fail to obey. Though both sides of this debate have a good array of arguments to support their causes, it is my contention that both views are correct; yet, at the same time, they both miss the mark.

There is a sense in which we do not even need to address the Christian Zionist's argument. We could simply agree with their claim that God will fulfill his promise of land to the people of God. We would then note that the fulfillment has already come in Christ. God fulfilled his promise, just as he said. After all, Jesus is the true descendant of Abraham and his ministry

---

2. It is important to understand the distinction between a promise that is tied to the covenant and one that is not. God's warning to Nineveh contained in the book of Jonah is an example of a prophecy that was not related to the covenant. God never had a covenant relationship with Nineveh. On the other hand, God's promises to Abraham of land and family are directly related to his covenant with Abraham. God promised Abraham these as a part of the covenant pledge. I will elaborate on this below. This distinction is important. In the case of a promise, such as those contained in the book of Jonah related to Nineveh, which is not tied to a covenant, they are wholly conditional. As for a promise, such as those made to Abraham regarding the land, which is directly related to the covenant, it is unconditional—though there are conditional elements.

3. Teplinsky, *Why Care About Israel?*, 27.

4. Pawson, *Defending Christian Zionism*, 49–50.

5. Horner, *Future Israel*, 238.

was a call to repent and return to the land.[6] The fulfillment of the land has come in Christ.[7]

The solution, however, is not quite that simple.[8] The first problem is that the question of whether or not God's promises to Abraham were conditional or unconditional is not an adequate question. The promise of land to Abraham cannot be understood as necessarily either/or.[9] The covenant promises have elements that are conditional and elements that are not conditional.[10]

6. Mark 1:2–3 opens with a citation of Isa 40:3 (and Mal 3:1 and Exod 23:20), which is a summons for the people of God to repent and return to the land. That Jesus was proclaiming that the restoration of God's people and the land was happening in Christ is fundamental to the Gospels.

7. See chap. 7 for a detailed defense of this position.

8. Note: The remainder of this chapter and the one to follow will be necessarily more complex. If what I said thus far works for you and if you find the material that follows to be too deep, then one can move forward. The crux of the matter is that the promises of land were fulfilled in Christ. The material that follows, however, has a number of necessary clarifications.

9. This is similar to the common assumption that the promises must be fulfilled either by Israel (literally) or the church (spiritually). When one creates these *either/or* conundrums it forces the reader to choose. The difficulty is that each side has good evidence to support their positions. The readers then usually opt for the side for which they are most familiar. The fact is, however, that there is good evidence for both sides. This is because many of these *either/or* suppositions are not truly either/or. They are often both/and. For example, with regard to whether or not the prophecies of land are fulfilled by *either* Israel *or* Jesus and the church we saw that it was both: Jesus is Israel and the beginning of the church. These two options cannot be separated. That is, today Israel, as the people of God, is the church (i.e., the NT people of God). This creates a tension that most tend to overlook. Many are not comfortable with acknowledging a *both/and*. After all, we expect God to make things neat and tidy—even though Scripture is clear that God's ways transcend ours (Isa 55:8–9). With regard to the covenants being conditional or unconditional, we shall see that they are both. There are clear conditional elements and clear unconditional elements. To argue that the covenants are *either* conditional *or* unconditional is to fail to fully understand the nature of the covenants.

10. The issue is further complicated by the fact that the promise of land is made twice. It was made first to Abraham. Then, after his descendants were sent off the land and into exile, the prophets reiterate the promise of land when they set forth the promise that God will restore the people of God to the land. Now, the biblical story includes the fact that the people of God were expelled from the land by God because of their disobedience. While they were in exile (that is, out of the land) the latter prophets provide encouragement to the people of God by informing them that God would restore them to the land. So when discussing the promise of land we have to address both the initial promise of land to Abraham as well as the later promises of the restoration of the land according to the prophets. To claim that the creation of the modern state of Israel is a

Promises as Conditional

The nature of God's promises in general are that they are conditional. God may well promise a nation blessings or curses and then not follow through with them. In doing so, God is not reneging on his promises or being unfaithful to his word. The fact is that God informs people or nations of his intent to bless or curse because he wants them to respond in a certain manner. Thus, when the prophets inform the people of God's plan, they do so because they want the people to act in a particular manner (most often they want the people to repent). If, on the one hand, the people obey and act as the prophet exhorts them, then God will bless them accordingly and/or he will relent in his intent to bring curses. If, on the other hand, the people fail to obey the prophet, then God will either relent on his promise of blessing and/or he will carry out his promise of curses.

This is made explicit by the prophet Jeremiah:

> Then the word of the LORD came to me saying, "Can I not, O house of Israel, deal with you as this potter *does*?" declares the LORD. "Behold, like the clay in the potter's hand, so are you in My hand, O house of Israel. At one moment I might speak concerning a nation or concerning a kingdom to uproot, to pull down, or to destroy *it*; if that nation against which I have spoken turns from its evil, I will relent concerning the calamity I planned to bring on it. Or at another moment I might speak concerning a nation or concerning a kingdom to build up or to plant *it*; if it does evil in My sight by not obeying My voice, then I will think better of the good with which I had promised to bless it." (Jer 18:5–10)

This principle is further exemplified in the promise to David and Solomon in 1 Kings. There they are promised that they will inherit the throne forever: "But King Solomon shall be blessed, and the throne of David shall be established before the LORD forever" (1 Kgs 2:45). At first look, we see no reason to assume that this is anything other than a promise of God that must be fulfilled. However, it does not take long to see that David and Solomon's empire is soon crushed by foreign invasions. The throne of David and Solomon does not last forever.[11]

Did God waver on his word or on his promise? No. The fact is that the promise was clearly conditional. That is, in order for David's throne to be

---

fulfillment of the promises of land we would need to ask: Which promise? The promise to Abraham, or the promise of restoration as found in the prophets?

11. There is a sense in which it does last forever in Jesus.

established forever, David and his descendants must remain faithful to the Lord. That this was clearly understood is evidenced by that fact that David himself exhorts his son Solomon just before he dies:

> I am going the way of all the earth. Be strong, therefore, and show yourself a man. Keep the charge of the LORD your God, to walk in His ways, to keep His statutes, His commandments, His ordinances, and His testimonies, according to what is written in the Law of Moses, *that* you may succeed in all that you do and wherever you turn, *so that* the LORD may carry out His promise which He spoke concerning me, saying, "If your sons are careful of their way, to walk before Me in truth with all their heart and with all their soul, you shall not lack a man on the throne of Israel." (1 Kgs 2:2–4)

Thus, the promise was conditional.

The simple fact is, then, that the nature of a promise of blessing or cursing is such that it was intended to motivate the people to act. This confirms that in general such promises are conditional. The promise may or may not take place depending on the conduct of the people. This is true regardless of whether or not a given promise states the conditions.[12]

The clear conditionality of prophecy is most evident in the prophecy of Jonah. The prophet Jonah was summoned to announce to the people of Nineveh, "Yet forty days and Nineveh will be overthrown" (Jonah 3:4). Now, if the nature of prophecy is such that it is inherently unconditional and that the prophecy must be fulfilled with a wooden literalism, then the meaning of the prophecy in Jonah is clear: Nineveh has forty days till its destruction. But if the nature of prophecy is such that it functions primarily to provoke a response of obedience (or continued obedience) to God, then the result may be different.

The story of Jonah clearly affirms the latter. For the text continues,

> Then the people of Nineveh believed in God; and they called a fast and put on sackcloth from the greatest to the least of them. When the word reached the king of Nineveh, he arose from his throne, laid aside his robe from him, covered *himself* with sackcloth and sat on the ashes. He issued a proclamation and it said, "In Nineveh by the decree of the king and his nobles: Do not let man, beast, herd, or flock taste a thing. Do not let them eat or drink water. But

---

12. A parent may promise a child that they will make cookies for dessert later that evening. However, when the evening rolls around and it turns out that the child was disobedient and refused to eat his/her dinner, the parent may well determine that they will not in fact make cookies.

both man and beast must be covered with sackcloth; and let men call on God earnestly that each may turn from his wicked way and from the violence which is in his hands." (Jonah 3:5–8)

Why did the people of Nineveh do this? Because they thought, "Who knows, God may turn and relent and withdraw His burning anger so that we will not perish" (Jonah 3:9).

The prophecy of Jonah invoked a response. That response was indeed the intent of the prophecy. The result: "When God saw their deeds, that they turned from their wicked way, then God relented concerning the calamity which He had declared He would bring upon them. And He did not do *it*" (Jonah 3:10). It is important to note that there was nothing in the prophecy to Nineveh itself to suggest that God would "change his mind" or alter his decision. The prophecy is put forward quite clearly. This is what God is about to do and this is the time frame in which he will do it. But God relents—even though it was never stated that he might relent.

We see from all of this that a fundamental aspect of prophecy is its conditional nature. God communicates his intent in order to facilitate a response on the part of the people.[13] The response of the people then dictates whether or not God will carry out the promised blessings or curses.

Does this all mean then that the promises to Abraham and the people of Israel that God would give them the land were conditional? Well, yes and no. They are conditional in the sense that in order for Abraham or any of his descendants to receive the blessings of the covenant, such as land, they must obey.[14] This is evident in that if Abraham does not obey the first part of the command and "go . . . to the land which I will show you" (Gen 12:1), then he would never receive any of the promises related to the covenant. Abraham must obey and do his part. He must "go."

This is true for any person or nation. This conditionality of the promises of blessing associated with the covenant is abundantly clear throughout the OT. For in the introduction to the Ten Commandments, which are the essence of the covenant obligations for the people, God declares, "'Now

---

13. There is more to this discussion that could be set forth. Though most prophecies are conditional in nature, there are some instances in which there are no conditionalities at all—namely, those prophecies that are accompanied by an oath or some sort of assurance from God; "thus says the Lord" (cf. Jer 7:15–6; 11:14; Amos 1:3, 6, 9, 13; 2:1, 4, 6; 4:2; 6:8; 8:7; Isa 54:9; Jer 44:26; Isa 62:8). These prophecies appear to have no conditionality: that is, they will come to pass regardless of how the people respond.

14. A covenant is a binding agreement between two parties. In the case of the OT, the covenant was between God and Israel (the people of God).

then, if you will indeed obey My voice and keep My covenant, then you shall be My own possession among all the peoples, for all the earth is Mine; and you shall be to Me a kingdom of priests and a holy nation.' These are the words that you shall speak to the sons of Israel" (Exod 19:5–6). Thus, the very introduction to the covenant speaks of conditionality. In order for the people of God to become "a kingdom of priests and a holy nation" they must "keep my covenant."

This conditionality of the covenant promises are affirmed in both Leviticus 26 and Deuteronomy 28—two passages that detail God's promises of blessings and curses associated with covenant obedience and covenant breaking for the people of Israel. In both passages, the blessings and curses of the covenant are wholly contingent on the obedience, or lack thereof, of the people. Leviticus 26 states, "If you walk in My statutes and keep My commandments . . . then I shall . . ." (Lev 26:3–4), and, "But if you do not obey . . . I, in turn, will do this to you . . ." (Lev 26:14–16).[15]

We see, then, that the covenant and its promises of blessing (and cursing) are inherently conditional. If it were simply a matter of either conditional or unconditional, then the issue might be considered closed. But it is not that simple.

Promises as Unconditional

It is the ardent contention of Christian Zionists that the promises to Abraham and his descendants regarding the land and the continuance of his family are unconditional.

Christian Zionist Michael Rydelnik claims that the promise of land was not dependent on Israel's faithfulness: "One of the essential principles of the Abrahamic covenant is that it is unconditional and eternal. Abraham did not need to do anything to receive or maintain this covenant."[16] Later he adds, "The land grant was both unconditional and eternal."[17]

Christian Zionists base their claim that God must fulfill the land promises on the assertion that they were unconditional. There is a truth here. It is not, however, simply because the promises were unconditional as the Christian Zionist claims. The Christian Zionist's failure to understand the role of Abraham and the OT people of God as the means by which God

15. Cp. 26:3–46; Deut 28, 30.

16. Rydelnik, *Understanding the Arab-Israeli Conflict*, 129.

17. Ibid., 157.

will bless the nations has obscured their understanding of the unconditional nature of the covenant promises.

The unconditional nature of the promises to Abraham derives from the fact that these promises are deeply related to the covenant. As such, they are not simply promises related to a single individual and his offspring. Instead, they are profoundly associated with God's plan of redemption for the nations.[18] The covenant promises relate to and are a vital part of the overall narrative of the biblical story. They are foundational elements of God's plan to redeem the nations. It is in this sense that the promises to Abraham must be fulfilled. The promises are unconditional in that God will be faithful to his covenant promises to carry out his mission of blessing all nations.

Consequently, the promises are both conditional—they are dependent upon Abraham and his offspring's continued obedience—and they are unconditional. John Walton notes,

> The revelatory program of the covenant stretches from Abraham to Christ. There is nothing conditional about this revelatory program: God is determined to reveal himself through the covenant and through Israel regardless of whether they are cooperative or faithful. But the formulation in Genesis 12 shows that there are two sides to the covenant. Abram's family has something to gain by being cooperative, thus the promises of land and family. These covenant benefits can be jeopardized by unfaithfulness. They can lose the land; they can be decimated as a nation. . . . Through Abram and his family all the people will receive blessing from God—this is the unconditional part. The benefits are conditional; God's revelatory program cannot be deterred.[19]

The Promises Are Both Conditional and Unconditional

We see then that the Replacement Theologians and the Christian Zionists are at the same time both correct and, yet, in error. The Replacement Theologian is correct when they assert that the promises of God are conditional. For, indeed, in order for Abraham or any particular person to experience the blessings of the covenant, they must be faithful to the covenant. The Christian Zionist is also correct when they note the unconditionally of the

18. Hence Gen 12:3, "And in you all the families of the earth will be blessed."

19. Walton, *Genesis*, 403.

covenants. For deep within the covenant promise of Genesis 12:1–3 is an unconditional promise of God that he will surely carry out—namely, that God fully intends to bring about the blessing of all nations and the entirety of the earth.

Both views are mistaken, however, because they fail to recognize the fundamental missional intent of God's redemptive plan to bless all the nations. Thus, contrary to the Replacement Theologian, the promise was unconditional: God will carry it out. At the same time, contrary to the Christian Zionist, Abraham and his descendants would personally receive the promised blessings of the covenant (especially land and family) only if they themselves remained faithful to the covenant.[20] Now God will bring

20. The Genesis narrative affirms the conditional element of the promises to Abraham: "By Myself I have sworn, declares the LORD, because you have done this thing and have not withheld your son, your only son, indeed I will greatly bless you, and I will greatly multiply your seed as the stars of the heavens and as the sand which is on the seashore; and your seed shall possess the gate of their enemies. In your seed all the nations of the earth shall be blessed, because you have obeyed My voice" (Gen 22:16–18). Some attempt to argue that since God swore on himself, the covenant is unconditional. But in this text we see that God's swearing is the result ("because," Gen 22:16, 18; cf. Gen 26:5) of Abraham's actions.

Christian Zionist Paul Benware cites Gen 22:16–18 along with Gen 17:1–2 and Gen 26:3–5 and acknowledges that "these passages seem to add conditions to the covenant." Benware, *Prophecy*, 42. Benware, however, denies that there are conditions to the original promise to Abraham. He responds by citing Renald Showers who claims that because Genesis 12 does not state any conditions to the covenant these later verses cannot be adding any conditions. Showers, *There Really Is a Difference*, 62, cited in Benware, *Prophecy*, 42.

There are several problems with Showers's argument. For one, we have already seen that Gen 12:1–3 contains conditions—Abraham is to "go" and if he does not go then the promise is null. One could argue that it is only speculation to say that if Abraham does not go, then the promise would not have been fulfilled. After all, since Abraham did go, we do not know what would have happened if he did not obey. This is true.

In addition, the fact that Gen 17, 22, and 26 all indicate that God blessed Abraham and that he will fulfill the covenant "because" Abraham obeyed. Therefore, it is clear that God blessed Abraham because he obeyed.

Furthermore, might we not understand Gen 17, 22, and 26 in terms of their affirming that such conditions were already present? Just because Gen 12 does not mention these conditions does not mean that they were not present. Thus, we can conclude that Gen 12 does not clearly state that the promise to Abraham was dependent on Abraham's obedience, but that Gen 17, 22, and 26 confirm that such was indeed the case.

Showers justifies his contention that no conditions can be added later by citing Gal 3:15 where Paul chides the Galatians for adding provisions to the covenant. Showers suggests that this means that no conditions may be added to the covenant. Okay, true. But this does not mean that the covenant has no conditions. Paul is condemning the Galatians for adding them. Gen 17, 22, and 26 are not adding conditions. These narratives

about the fulfillment of his promise. However, he will do so only through the faithful descendant of Abraham.

CONCLUSION: THE PROMISES ARE BOTH CONDITIONAL AND UNCONDITIONAL

The covenant promise to Abraham must be understood as both conditional and unconditional. Thus, contrary to the Replacement Theologian, who asserts that the covenant was conditional and that Israel's disobedience meant that God rejected Israel, we find that Jesus and the NT people of God are not a replacement of Israel, but the fulfillment of Israel. The promise was unconditional in that it was tied to God's redemptive plan, which he will bring about. The Replacement Theologian is seriously mistaken when it is asserted that Israel failed so God appointed Jesus and the church. Israel did not ultimately fail. For Jesus is Israel.

At the same time, contrary to the claims of the Christian Zionist that the promise was unconditional, we see that all such promises are conditional. The promise of blessing was dependent on the faithfulness of Abraham and his descendants. It was not going to be fulfilled unless they were faithful.[21] This points us to Jesus—He was the faithful Israel! God was going to fulfill his promises. And he did—through Jesus.

Therefore, contrary to Replacement Theology, the promises of God in Genesis 12:1–3 to Abraham and his descendants have not been "transferred" to Jesus and the church who "replace" Israel. They have been fulfilled in Jesus, but not in rejection of Israel. To suggest that the promises were fulfilled by Jesus and the church apart from the fulfillment of God's

---

are confirming for us that the covenant already had such conditions. Showers fails to recognize then that Gen 17, 22, and 26 are not adding conditions to the covenant of Gen 12. They merely confirm that conditions were already clearly in place. It is somewhat ironic here that one of the major principles set forth by Benware, Walvoord, Showers, and almost all dispensationalists and Christian Zionists is the notion of "Progressive Revelation" (see Benware, Walvoord). Progressive Revelation says that later revelation serves to clarify earlier revelations. For example, the OT does not teach with any level of clarity the triune nature of God. However, that God is triune is very evident from the NT. The latter revelation of the NT with regard to the Trinity is then used to highlight the more obscure passages on the nature of God in the OT. Why, then, cannot we do the same with the covenant? May we not conclude that Gen 17, 22, and 26, which clearly inform us of the conditional nature of the covenant, clarify for us that the covenant with Abraham in Gen 12 was conditional?

21. I will elaborate on this point in the following chapter.

promises to Abraham is to deny the fundamental nature of Jesus as the true Israel. It also denies the continuity between the OT and the NT. Furthermore, it fails to understand the purpose and nature of God's redemptive promises and his desire to bless all mankind throughout the entire earth.

At the same time, the Christian Zionist's claim that the promises to Abraham were unconditional and that they await a future fulfillment in the physical, ethnic nation of Israel cut across the grain of everything we see in Scripture. Covenant blessing is wholly tied to covenant obedience. To claim that these promises are unconditional and that they must be fulfilled by the physical, ethnic descendants of Abraham regardless of their faithfulness to God's commands contradicts everything we know of the nature of covenant promises. In addition, to suggest that the promises to Abraham await a future fulfillment in the physical, ethnic descendants of Abraham alone, fails to recognize that these promises have already been fulfilled in Jesus—the true ethnic descendant of Abraham and the true Israel.

It is not a question, then, with regard to the promises of family and land to Abraham, of whether the covenant is conditional or unconditional. It is clearly both. The promise to Abraham, that God will bless Abraham and all the nations, is unconditional. It is part of God's sovereign plan of redemption. At the same time the promise is clearly conditional. Abraham must "go" or he will not inherit the land. This is why Scripture affirms, "because you have done this . . . indeed I will greatly bless you, and I will greatly multiply your seed" (Gen 22:16–17). For Abraham, or any particular person, to inherit the blessings of the covenant they must remain faithful.

Chapter 13

Were the Promises to Abraham "Forever"?

[There is] no instance where Jesus expects a fulfilment of Old Testament prophecy other than through his own ministry, and certainly no suggestion of a future restoration of the Jewish nation independent of himself. He is the fulfilment to which prophecy points.[1]

If, as suggested above, Jesus was claiming to be, in effect, the new or true temple, and if his death is to be seen as the drawing together into one of the history of Israel in her desolation, dying her death outside the walls of the city, and rising again as the beginning of the real "restoration," the real return from exile, then the attempt to say that there are some parts of the OT (relating to Jerusalem, Land, or Temple) which have not been "fulfilled" and so need a historical and literal "fulfillment" now, or at some other time, is an explicit attempt to take something away from the achievement of Christ in his death and resurrection, and to reserve it for the work of human beings in a different time and place.[2]

1. France, "OT Prophecy and the Future of Israel," 58. See C. Wright, "Christian Approach," 10.
2. Walker, *Jerusalem Past and Present*, 74.

In addition to their claim that the promise of land to Abraham was unconditional, the Christian Zionist argues that the promise of land must be
fulfilled in the future by ethnic Israel because it was given to them by God
as an "everlasting possession" (Gen 17:8).[3] As Christian Zionist Michael
Rydelnik claims,

> God has granted the title deed of the land of Israel to the Jewish
> people. . . . The land grant was both unconditional and eternal.
> Although the Jewish people might be disciplined with dispersion,
> their right to the land will never be removed.[4]

Christian Zionist David Stern states emphatically,

> The promise of the land of Israel is forever, and the plain sense of
> this is that the Jewish people will possess the land (at least in trust-
> eeship) and live there. To say that the New Covenant transforms
> this plain sense into an assertion that those who believe in Yeshua
> come into some vague spiritual "possession" or a spiritual "terri-
> tory" is intellectual sleight of hand aiming at denying, canceling
> and reducing to naught a real promise given to real people in the
> real world.[5]

The Christian Zionist then claims that since the physical/ethnic descendants of Abraham have yet to dwell in the land "forever," the promise
must have a future fulfillment. Though the theological implications are
great, the repercussions for the present conflict are enormous. On the surface, this appears to be a quite formidable argument.

The response is actually quite simple. As argued throughout this book,
these promises are fulfilled in Jesus. Jesus is the true "seed" of Abraham
(Gal 3:16). Through Jesus, the people of God are inheriting not just the land
of promise, but the whole "world" (Rom 4:13). This fulfillment will indeed
be everlasting. After all, God never intended the land to be restricted to one
place. The glory of God was always intended to fill the earth (Isa 6:3).

---

3. The NASB, ESV, NIV, and NKJV all render this as "everlasting possession." The
NET Bible renders it a "permanent possession" and the NLT reads "possession forever."
Kaiser repeatedly notes that the covenant is "a *perpetual* covenant" (emphasis original).
Kaiser, "Land of Israel and the Future Return (Zechariah 10:6–12)," in House, *Israel, the
Land and the People*, 209. He also refers to it as "irrevocability" (211); "immutable" (211);
"eternal promise" (211); and "*eternal*" (211).

4. Rydelnik, *Understanding the Arab-Israeli Conflict*, 126, 157.

5. David Stern, cited by Lisa Loden, "Assessing the Various Hermeneutical Approaches," in *Bible and the Land*, 24–25.

We would do well to close the argument at this point. We have already noted repeatedly that the Scriptures are about Jesus, that Jesus is the true Israel, and that all of God's promises are fulfilled in him.

When it comes to the land promises, however, the issue is not quite that simple. For the Christian Zionist has failed to recognize, as we will see below, that the promises of land to Abraham and his descendants were actually fulfilled in the pages of the OT. This fact will complicate matters for a bit. For it raises the question "If these promises were fulfilled in the OT itself, then in what sense were they fulfilled by Jesus?"

The answer brings us back to our discussion in chapter 7 of the nature and purpose of the land promises. Though the land promises find their fulfillment with the pages of the OT itself, we realize that the purpose of those promises were not fulfilled. That is, God's desire to bless all nations throughout the entire earth, which was to last forever, is what the NT claims was fulfilled in Jesus.

THE MEANING OF OLAM ("EVERLASTING"; "FOREVER")

As mentioned above, the OT presents us with a dilemma when it comes to the possession of the land of promise by the descendants Abraham— namely, that God promises Abraham and his offspring the land forever: "And I will give to you and to your descendants after you, the land of your sojournings, all the land of Canaan, for an everlasting possession; and I will be their God" (Gen 17:8). The problem is that they do not seem to possess it forever. It is here that the Christian Zionist asserts that the Jewish people must be restored to the land in the future in order to fulfill this promise.

One problem with this reasoning, however, is that the Hebrew word *olam* ("forever"; or "everlasting") does not always mean "forever" as the English translations may suggest. There are many instances in the OT where *olam* does not connote "forever" in the strictest sense.[6] Christopher Wright comments, "The expression 'for ever' needs to be seen, not so much in terms of 'everlastingness' in linear time, but rather as an intensive expression within the terms, conditions and context of the promise concerned.

---

6. A few instances in which the Hebrew *olam* does not mean "everlasting" in the strict literal sense include: Aaronic Levites are to serve as priests "forever" (Exod 29:9; 1 Chron 23:13); David's descendants will be enthroned "forever" (2 Sam 7:12–16); and the Rechabites were to last "forever" (Jer 35:18–19). See Walton, *Genesis*, 450.

'For ever' is not, in Hebrew, as infinite as it sounds in English."[7] Peter Walker adds, "Perhaps the Hebrew word forever (*le'olam*) does not mean literally 'to the end of the eternity' but only 'for a very long time.'"[8] Even the Christian Zionist writer Michael Rydelnik acknowledges, "It is possible that the Hebrew word used in these passages (*olam*) and translated 'forever' does not necessarily mean 'for all eternity.'"[9]

This creates a significant problem for the Christian Zionist. For if *olam* does not necessarily mean "into all eternity," then the Christian Zionist's assertion that the land belongs to the Jewish people as a possession into all eternity disappears. For if the promise was only that the descendants of Abraham would inherit the land for a very long time, then perhaps the "literal" fulfillment has already come. After all, Abraham and his offspring held the land for a long time.

WHEN WOULD THE PROMISE END?

If the promise of land was only for a long time and not "forever," then what might constitute the end of this promise? It is my contention, as has been argued at length in this book, that the land was only intended to serve as the exclusive place of God's dwelling among the descendants of Abraham until the fulfillment came. Once the fulfillment came—i.e., once the land had accomplished its purpose as the place from which God would bless all lands—the grand purpose of the land finds its fulfillment—namely, the whole earth becomes more and more the place of God's dwelling. As already discussed at some length, this is precisely what we see in the NT.

Consequently, the Christian Zionist's argument that the land was promised to Abraham and his offspring as an "everlasting possession" is deeply flawed. The promise was never intended to be theirs alone forever in the sense of "without end." It was only theirs alone until the fulfillment came.[10]

7. Wright, "Christian Approach," in *Jerusalem Past and Present*, 6.

8. Walker, introduction to *Gospel and the Land of Promise*, 4.

9. Rydelnik, *Understanding the Arab-Israeli Conflict*, 155. He adds, "Nevertheless, the promise of God as recorded in the Scriptures indicates Israel's ownership or title to the land remains eternal and unconditional. It belongs to them for all time because the land grant was not dependent on Israel's obedience but on God's faithfulness to His oath" (157).

10. Walter Kaiser, who supports Christian Zionism, acknowledges, "But an even more important point must be made. The promise of the coming Seed (eventually to be

WAS THE PROMISE TO ABRAHAM FULFILLED?

In addition to the problems stated above, the Christian Zionist's assertion that the promise of the land to the descendants of Abraham must be fulfilled in the future by ethnic Israelites fails to account for the testimony of the OT itself. What the Christian Zionist often overlooks is the fact that within the OT itself the promises to Abraham, both regarding his family and the land, are acknowledged as having been fulfilled.[11]

That the OT understands the promise of land to Abraham and his descendants as fulfilled is evidenced by the statement in Joshua 21:

> So the LORD gave Israel all the land which He had sworn to give to their fathers, and they possessed it and lived in it. And the LORD gave them rest on every side, according to all that He had sworn to their fathers, and no one of all their enemies stood before them; the LORD gave all their enemies into their hand. Not one of the good promises which the LORD had made to the house of Israel failed; all came to pass. (Josh 21:43–45)

The text is clear. The promises of land are seen as fulfilled in the settling of the Israelites in the land of Canaan after the forty years of wilderness wanderings.

In addition, we see in Deuteronomy that the promise of descendants to Abraham are fulfilled. Deuteronomy states: "Your fathers went down to Egypt seventy persons *in all*, and now the LORD your God has made you as numerous as the stars of heaven" (Deut 10:22). The significance of this citation is that it is clearly alluding to the promise in Genesis as evidenced by the reiteration of the promise to Abraham that his descendants will be as numerous as the stars.[12]

---

known as the Messiah) and the offer of the good news (i.e., that in Abraham's seed all the nations of the earth would be blessed) was inextricably tied to the promise of land." Kaiser, "Land of Israel and the Future Return (Zechariah 10:6–12)," in House, *Israel, the Land and the People*, 211. What is somewhat perplexing here is that Kaiser would affirm that the promise of the coming Seed has arrived in Christ. So why would he not also acknowledge that the fulfillment of land must also have come in Christ?

11. As stated above, it is important to understand that the promise of land may have been fulfilled prior to the purpose of the land being fulfilled. That is, God promised to give the descendants of Abraham the land. This he did—as we will see. The purpose of the land, however, which was to be the place from which God blesses the whole earth, came in Christ.

12. Cf. Gen 15:5; 22:17; 26:4; 32:12.

Therefore, to claim that the Holy Land must be restored to the Jewish people today in order that God's promises may be fulfilled is a failure to acknowledge that the promise itself has already been fulfilled. What was yet to be fulfilled by the end of the OT was the purpose for the promise.[13] In Jesus the very purpose of the promise finds its fulfillment.

WHY WAS ISRAEL EXPELLED FROM THE LAND BEFORE THE FULFILLMENT?

Someone may well respond by asking why, if God only intended to give the land to Israel until the fulfillment came, they lost possession of the land before the fulfillment came? That is, if the fulfillment came in Jesus, why were the descendants of Abraham sent out of the land and into exile hundreds of years before Christ?[14]

The reason for the loss of the land by Abraham's descendants is tied to covenant faithfulness. Their possession of the land was conditional and in direct correlation to their faithfulness to God's commands. This is clearly seen in a number of passages in the OT, but most particularly in Deuteronomy and Leviticus. Deuteronomy, in fact, states that the people of Israel will lose the land when they are not faithful:

> When you become the father of children and children's children and have remained long in the land, and act corruptly, and make an idol in the form of anything, and do that which is evil in the sight of the LORD your God *so as* to provoke Him to anger, I call heaven and earth to witness against you today, that you will surely perish quickly from the land where you are going over the Jordan to possess it. You shall not live long on it, but will be utterly destroyed. The LORD will scatter you among the peoples, and you will be left few in number among the nations where the LORD drives you. (Deut 4:25–27)

---

13. This is why the prophets reiterate the promise of land and family. That is, although they recognized that in a basic sense the promises were fulfilled, they understood that the promises pointed to something beyond. That is, the promises pointed to a time when all the nations and all the earth would be blessed. For that to take place someone greater than Jacob (John 4:12), the temple (Matt 12:6), Jonah (Matt 12:41; Luke 11:32), Solomon (Matt 12:42; Luke 11:31), and Abraham (John 8:53) must come!

14. The northern kingdom of Israel was sent out of the land by the Assyrians in 721BC and the southern kingdom of Judah was sent out of the land by the Babylonians in 586BC.

Later, in Deuteronomy 28 the blessings and the curses associated with faithfulness to the covenant are catalogued. Note the relationship of covenant faithfulness to the blessings and the land:

> Now it shall be, if you diligently obey the LORD your God, being careful to do all His commandments which I command you today, the LORD your God will set you high above all the nations of the earth. All these blessings will come upon you and overtake you if you obey the LORD your God: Blessed *shall* you *be* in the city, and blessed *shall* you *be* in the country. . . . The LORD shall cause your enemies who rise up against you to be defeated before you; they will come out against you one way and will flee before you seven ways. The LORD will command the blessing upon you in your barns and in all that you put your hand to, and He will bless you in the land which the LORD your God gives you. . . . The LORD will make you abound in prosperity, in the offspring of your body and in the offspring of your beast and in the produce of your ground, in the land which the LORD swore to your fathers to give you. The LORD will open for you His good storehouse, the heavens, to give rain to your land in its season and to bless all the work of your hand; and you shall lend to many nations, but you shall not borrow. . . . If you listen to the commandments of the LORD your God, which I charge you today, to observe *them* carefully, and do not turn aside from any of the words which I command you today, to the right or to the left, to go after other gods to serve them." (Deut 28:1–14)

In the same way the curses for disobedience are intimately tied to the land. The ultimate curse for covenant disobedience, in fact, comes in the form of being expelled from the land:

> But it shall come about, if you do not obey the LORD your God, to observe to do all His commandments and His statutes with which I charge you today, that all these curses will come upon you and overtake you: Cursed *shall* you *be* in the city, and cursed *shall* you *be* in the country. . . . The LORD will make the rain of your land powder and dust; from heaven it shall come down on you until you are destroyed. The LORD shall cause you to be defeated before your enemies; you will go out one way against them, but you will flee seven ways before them, and you will be *an example of* terror to all the kingdoms of the earth. . . . You shall bring out much seed to the field but you will gather in little, for the locust will consume it. You shall plant and cultivate vineyards, but you will neither drink of the wine nor gather *the grapes*, for the worm will devour

them. You shall have olive trees throughout your territory but you will not anoint yourself with the oil, for your olives will drop off. . . . Moreover, the LORD will scatter you among all peoples, from one end of the earth to the other end of the earth; and there you shall serve other gods, wood and stone, which you or your fathers have not known. Among those nations you shall find no rest, and there will be no resting place for the sole of your foot; but there the LORD will give you a trembling heart, failing of eyes, and despair of soul. (Deut 28:15–16, 24–25, 38–40, 64–65)

The relationship between the faithfulness of the people of God and the possession of the land is iterated in Leviticus as well. According to Leviticus, the people are to be faithful so that:

The land will not spew you out, should you defile it, as it has spewed out the nation which has been before you." (Lev 18:28)

Now it should be noted that the relationship between covenant faithfulness and the land was not some later addition. It was present from the beginning of God's promises to Abraham. Genesis 17:8–10 ties the promise of land to covenant faithfulness:

"I will give to you and to your descendants after you, the land of your sojournings, all the land of Canaan, for an everlasting possession; and I will be their God." God said further to Abraham, "Now as for you, you shall keep My covenant, you and your descendants after you throughout their generations. This is My covenant, which you shall keep, between Me and you and your descendants after you."

Therefore, the promise of land to Abraham and his descendants cannot be disassociated from the faithfulness of the people of God. Though they were intended to possess the land until the time of the fulfillment, that is Christ, they were expelled from the land prior to this time because they were unfaithful. The land did not belong to Abraham and his descendants because God simply made some "everlasting" promise to them.[15] These

---

15. Technically, the land never belonged to Abraham and his descendants. The land belongs to Yahweh and they were tenants upon it. Therefore, the contention of Rydelnik that "the Jewish people may indeed temporarily lose the enjoyment and habitation of the land of Israel, but they can never lose the title deed to the land" is false. See Rydelnik, *Understanding the Arab-Israeli Conflict*, 158. The fact is that they never had title deed to the land. Yahweh owns the land! "In a profound sense, Israel never 'owns' the land of promise. *God owns this land*." Burge, *Jesus and the Land*, 4. This explains why they were never permitted to sell the land. They did not own it. See also C. Wright, *Mission*.

promises were conditional and dependent upon the faithfulness of the people.

The question then arises as to how Jesus could be the fulfillment of the promise of land when the faithlessness of the people effectively broke the covenant. The answer is found in God's desire to bring redemption to the nations.

WHY THE PROPHETS PROMISE A RESTORATION TO THE LAND

After the descendants of Abraham broke the covenant and were expelled from the land, God promised out of his mercy to return the people to the land. These promises were not based on some binding promise by which God was required to act in order to be faithful to Abraham and Israel. Instead, God's promises of restoration were a result of his desire to bring about the redemption of the nations. That is, the very reason why he chose Abraham and his descendants, that they might be a light and the source of blessing to the nations, was the basis from which he promised that he would bring his descendants back to the land.

This confirms that God's actions towards Israel have never been for the sake of Israel alone. God has always had as the center of his redemptive will the redemption of all creation and all humankind.[16] The fact that the land promises were to be fulfilled in Christ stems from God's desire to bring about the redemption of the nations and not some binding obligation towards the ethnic descendants of Abraham alone. Consequently, after the Israelites were expelled from the land the latter prophets arise and promise the restoration of the temple, the land, and the people of Israel.

The question, then, of the restoration of temple, land, and people is not bound with some irrevocable promise of God, as though God never fulfilled his promises to Abraham and, consequently, now he must do so. The promises to Abraham were fulfilled. That they did not remain in the land was directly related to the disobedience of the people. It was after the descendants of Abraham were expelled from the land that the latter prophets arose and declared that God would again restore the temple and the land, and bring the people back.

16. This, however, runs counter to almost every assumption of Christian Zionism. For the Christian Zionist, God's acts towards Israel are for the sake of Israel alone.

It is primarily these prophecies regarding the restoration of the land that really need to be the focus of discussion with the Christian Zionists. The prophets were not saying that God will restore you to the land and rebuild your temple because he never really fulfilled his promises to Abraham. What was yet to be fulfilled was the purpose for which God called Abraham to the land. What had not yet been accomplished was the redeeming of all nations, all lands, and the restoration of God's presence among all people.

Herein lies another foundational misunderstanding on the part of the Christian Zionists. They assume that the restoration of the temple, people, and land are to fulfill the *promises* of God rather than the *purpose* of God. The promises of God have been fulfilled as announced within the OT itself. Because the Christian Zionists have failed to recognize that the promises have been fulfilled, it is not surprising that they are awaiting a fulfillment in terms that look like the OT promises themselves. When the OT closes with the promise of a restoration of the people and the land it is in accord with the purpose of God to bless all nations and all lands.

The Christian Zionists are looking for a fulfillment that benefits the nation of Israel alone. This fulfillment has already come according to the OT. The fulfillment that the latter portions of the OT then promise is in relation to the reestablishing of the people of God and the land so that by it God might bless the nations. And it is this fulfillment that the NT affirms has occurred in Jesus.

RESTORATION ACCORDING TO THE PROPHETS

What the latter prophets are looking forward to when they speak of the restoration of the people of God and the land is that the purpose of God in blessing the nations will be fulfilled. That is why Ezekiel proclaims,

> My servant David will be king over them, and they will all have one shepherd; and they will walk in My ordinances and keep My statutes and observe them. They will live on the land that I gave to Jacob My servant, in which your fathers lived; and they will live on it, they, and their sons and their sons' sons, forever; and David My servant will be their prince forever. I will make a covenant of peace with them; it will be an everlasting covenant with them. And I will place them and multiply them, and will set My sanctuary in their midst forever. My dwelling place also will be with them; and I will be their God, and they will be My people. And the nations will

know that I am the LORD who sanctifies Israel, when My sanctuary is in their midst forever. (Ezek 37:24–28)

Notice that Ezekiel refers to the restoration in terms of four features that are of particular interest to us: first, there is the restoration of the Davidic kingdom; second, they will walk according to God's law; third, the people will return to the land; finally, God's temple presence will be with them.

Though this passage may, at first sight, suggest the restoration of a Davidic kingdom similar to what it was at the time of David, we quickly realize that the prophet has a far more magnificent picture in view. A look at these four features of the restoration confirms that they are fulfilled in Jesus and in a manner that transcends the "literal."[17]

First, we know from the NT that Jesus is the Davidic King.[18] And though his kingdom is not of this world,[19] he will continue to rule until he possesses the entire creation.[20]

What is not always as well understood is that the second feature in Ezekiel's prophecy, the presence of God's law within his people, is already being fulfilled. The NT affirms that through the Spirit the law of God is now written on the hearts of the NT people of God. This is what the author of Hebrews makes explicit when he states,

> For by one offering He has perfected for all time those who are sanctified. And the Holy Spirit also testifies to us; for after saying, "This is the covenant that I will make with them after those days, says the Lord: I will put my laws upon their heart, and on their mind I will write them," He then says, "And their sins and their lawless deeds I will remember no more." Now where there is forgiveness of these things, there is no longer any offering for sin. (Heb 10:14–18)

The point the author of Hebrews is making is that Christ has indeed offered the one perfect sacrifice, and as a result of that sacrifice God has established his everlasting covenant with the people of God—though the author of Hebrews is citing the covenant promise of Jeremiah 31:31–33,

---

17. Again, the word "literal" begs to be defined. I use it here in accord with the meaning that Christian Zionists often assume.

18. John 18:37; 1 Tim 1:17; 6:15; Rev 15:3; 17:14; 19:16.

19. John 18:36.

20. 1 Cor 15:20–28.

the point remains the same as in Ezekiel 37—namely, that God's everlasting covenant of peace has been established with his people through Christ.

Skipping for the moment to the fourth feature, we again note that the promise that God will dwell among his people is presently fulfilled by means of the indwelling presence of the Holy Spirit in the life of the people of God. Paul affirms this when he cites Ezekiel 37 as fulfilled: "For we are the temple of the living God; just as God said, *'I will dwell in them and walk among them; and I will be their God and they shall be my people'*" (2 Cor 6:16).[21]

That the third feature of Ezekiel's prophecy, the restoration of the land, is also fulfilled in the NT people of God is also evidenced by the fact that Paul cites this passage as fulfilled by Christ. For, if each of the other elements are fulfilled in Christ, then it stands to reason that the promise of the restoration of land has been also. I have already argued at some length in chapter 7 that the land promises are fulfilled in the NT. If the promise of the restoration of the temple is fulfilled in the person of Christ, then why should we not also conclude that the promise of the restoration of the land is fulfilled in the person of Christ?

To suggest that this passage requires a literalistic fulfillment of the land contradicts every other fulfillment of this passage in the NT. We know that Jesus was crowned king forever. We also know that Christ became king on the cross—hardly what a literalistic fulfillment would have predicted. Even the promise of God's restoration of his temple presence among his people would most likely have conjured up expectations of some glorious building that shone brilliantly above Jerusalem. Instead, the fulfillment looked like a suffering savior on a cross, who then rose again on the third day and gave us his Spirit, thereby establishing his eternal temple presence.

Why then should we expect the restoration of the land to have some woodenly literalistic fulfillment? Everything we see here suggests that the fulfillment transcends the woodenly literal. This is not to say that the fulfillment is simply spiritual. Jesus is literally and physically the temple of God. And so are his people. The fulfillment of the temple transcends a building in Jerusalem. So also, then, the fulfillment of the promise of the restoration of the land transcends the physical Holy Land. Jesus is the temple. Jesus is the land. Jesus is the people of God. And so are those who are in Christ.

---

21. This citation of Paul's here is a composite citation of Lev 26:12 and Ezek 37:27.

CONCLUSION

In sum, then, the promise of land to Abraham and his descendants was ful-filled within the pages of the OT. The Christian Zionist claim that the land continues to belong to the physical/ethnic descendants of Abraham be-cause God gave it to them forever is mistaken. The land was never theirs. It was God's and they were tenants on it. The promise was not that they would possess it forever, but for a long time. And they did. Thus, those promises were fulfilled. They lived on the land. As Joshua says, "The Lord gave Israel all the land which he swore to give to their fathers, and they possessed it and lived in it" (Josh 21:43). In addition, they had "rest" from their enemies (Josh 21:44). As a result, "not one of the good promises which the LORD had made to the house of Israel failed; all came to pass" (Josh 21:45). What had not been fulfilled by the end of the pages of the OT was the purpose of God's giving them the land—namely, that it was to be the means by which God would bless the whole earth. It is this that was accomplished by Jesus.

Chapter 14

Was 1948 a Fulfillment of Prophecy?

I have argued at length that the Christian Zionist's assertion that the promises of land in Scripture are awaiting a future fulfillment[1] and the return of physical/ethnic descendants of Abraham to the land fails to understand that Jesus is Israel and that God's promises are fulfilled in him. At this point I find that many evangelicals are prepared to accept this conclusion. It makes sense of both the OT and the NT. But a significant question arises: "What about the events of 1948 and 1967?" Does not the restoration of the Jewish people and the modern state of Israel in the last century confirm that God has miraculously brought the people of Israel back?

WERE THE EVENTS OF 1948 AND 1967 A FULFILLMENT OF PROPHECY?

This is perhaps the most common—and to some extent persuasive—evidence in favor of the view that the promises of land to Israel must be fulfilled by the physical/ethnic descendants of Abraham. After more than two thousand years[2] and numerous tragic events, the climax of which was the

---

1. By "future" I mean from the perspective of the NT. Many Christian Zionists claim that these promises were fulfilled in 1948 and 1967.

2. The Jewish people had not experienced independence since the brief rule of the Hasmoneans in the second century BC.

Holocaust in Nazi Germany, the Jewish people finally gained a state and a land to call their own.

The restoration of the nation of Israel in the twentieth century is surely a phenomenon that appears to justify the Christian Zionist reading of the Bible. If the Bible prophesies that the nation of Israel will be restored and play a vital role in the events of the end-times, then surely the events of the last century appear to support this interpretation. The miraculousness of this occurrence has led many to assert that the birth of the modern state of Israel was none other than the hand of God. Rydelnik contends, "The best explanation is that the modern state of Israel seems to be a dramatic work of God in fulfillment of the Bible's predictions of a Jewish return to the land of Israel."[3]

This seems on the surface to be a formidable argument. The revival of the state of Israel in modern times is, indeed, an amazing set of events. But are these events fulfillments of prophecies? Do they prove that the prophecies of the restoration of the people and the land must be fulfilled in a literalistic fashion by the physical descendants of Abraham?

The answers to these questions are simply no. As amazing as these events are for the Jewish world, they do not have any effect on our understanding of Scripture. In saying this, I am in no way attempting to disparage the modern state of Israel or the Jewish people. I do not intend to deny the miraculousness of the recent events. Nor is this an attempt to diminish the strength and resolve of the Jewish people. I am only addressing the question from a biblical and theological perspective. From this perspective the promises to Israel were fulfilled by Christ.

To suggest that viewpoints such as mine leave no place for the Jewish people is to fail to understand the message. The point I wish to make is simply that the biblical restoration of Israel has come in Jesus and that this restoration includes the redemption of the nations. And, if the restoration includes the nations, then, surely this includes Israel. Jesus has come and brought redemption for all. "All" includes Jew and Gentile, slave and free, male and female (Gal 3:28). There is no one to whom the offer to join Christ at his banquet table does not include! As a result, the Jewish people have every right to join Christ at his banquet.

3. Rydelnik, *Understanding the Arab-Israeli Conflict*, 132.

JESUS UNDERSTOOD THE RESTORATION OF ISRAEL WAS THROUGH HIM

First, we must reiterate that the Bible's promise of the restoration of the people of Israel to the land has been fulfilled in Jesus. This is evident in the Gospel of Luke, which opens and closes with references to Jesus as the fulfillment of the restoration of Israel.[4] Christopher Wright notes that Luke 1–2 are "saturated with the motif of fulfillment of Old Testament prophecies about Israel."[5]

In addition, it is clear that Jesus employed texts that referred to the ingathering of Israel and applied them to his own ministry and the coming ingathering of the nations. For example, in Matthew 8:11, Jesus says,

> I say to you that many will come from east and west, and recline *at the table* with Abraham, Isaac and Jacob in the kingdom of heaven.

What is important to note here is that Jesus is citing a long tradition of Scriptures that address the hope of God's promised banquet with Abraham, Isaac, and Jacob.[6] Jesus announces that the promised end-times banquet for Israel is happening. He does so, however, in response to the faith of a centurion. His announcement of the presence of the end-times banquet includes the caveat that the nations are joining them. The result is that "in this way Jesus actually appears to redefine and extend the very meaning of the 'restoration of Israel' in terms of the Gentiles."[7]

That Jesus extends the end-times banquet to include the nations squares perfectly with the fact that God's purpose for choosing Abraham and his descendants was that through them he might bless the nations. This is crucial for our understanding. The promise of the restoration of Israel was already taking place in the ministry of Jesus. This restoration included the nations. That is, it was not restricted to the gathering of Israel alone. For,

---

4. Luke 1:68, 74; 24:21. In Luke 24 the two men on the road to Emmaus declare, "We were hoping that it was He who was going to redeem Israel" (24:21). This closing remark must be read in light of the declaration that Simeon was "looking for the consolation of Israel" (2:25) and that Anna was speaking to all "who were looking for the redemption of Jerusalem" (2:38).

5. C. Wright, "Christian Approach," 13.

6. Cf. Isa 43:5–6; 49:12; Ps 107:3; Mark 13:27—Deut 30:4; Zech 2:6—applies OT language referring to Israel (Ps 107:3; Isa 43:5–6; 49:12).

7. C. Wright, "Christian Approach," 15.

as we have seen, Israel was called to be the means by which God redeemed the nations. And this is precisely what Jesus and the NT announces.

THE PURPOSE OF THE RESTORATION OF ISRAEL: TO BE A LIGHT TO THE NATIONS

Another way of looking at the restoration of Israel is to understand that the people of God have been called *for* something and not simply *to* something. Abraham and his descendants were called *for* the sake of the nations: to be a light to them. Thus, Isaiah declares, "I am the LORD, I have called you in righteousness, I will also hold you by the hand and watch over you, and I will appoint you as a covenant to the people, as a light to the nations, To open blind eyes" (Isa 42:6–7a).

Throughout the OT we see that the people of God failed to carry out this mission. In fact, they could not carry it out because, as the prophets declared, Israel, like the nations, was also blind: "Who is blind but My servant, Or so deaf as My messenger whom I send? Who is so blind as he that is at peace *with Me*, Or so blind as the servant of the LORD?" (Isa 42:19). As a result, the OT people of God were themselves in need of someone who could open their eyes that they might see! Only then would they be able to carry out their mission.

It is in view of this larger purpose of being a light to the nations that Isaiah announces that God will restore Israel. The prophet acknowledges, "It is too small a thing that You should be My Servant To raise up the tribes of Jacob and to restore the preserved ones of Israel; I will also make You a light of the nations So that My salvation may reach to the end of the earth" (Isa 49:6). That is, if God restored Israel for the sake of Israel alone, that would be "too small a thing." God can do more than that. Therefore, Isaiah declares, God will restore Israel in order that Israel might also be a light to the nations.

The Christian Zionist, however, fails to consider the reason why God promised to restore the people of God. They assume that the physical nation of Israel is just special for its own sake and that God must keep his word. Once we realize that Israel—the OT people of God—was chosen for something—that God might be known to the nations—then we can begin to look at the NT and realize that this has already happened!

The Christian Zionists' claim that God will restore physical/ethnic Israel to the land as he promised fails, then, on a number of fronts. Primary

among them is that Christian Zionism does not understand that the restoration of the people of God was in order that they might fulfill their mission
of being a light to the nations. The failure to grasp this point is one of the
central reasons why Christian Zionism does not recognize that the fulfillment of the promises to Abraham and the OT people of God were fulfilled
in Jesus.

Christian Zionists then are looking for the fulfillment of the restoration of physical/ethnic Israel to the land and not in accordance with the
purposes of their restoration. Because Christian Zionism does not consider
this aspect, they are left looking for some supposed future "literal" fulfillment, which 1948 and 1967 then seems to fulfill. Jesus, however, accomplished the very purpose of the restoration of people of God to the land.
Consequently, 1948 and 1967 do not provide any measure of fulfillment in
regard to the promises of Scripture.

THE ROLE OF ISRAEL WAS FULFILLED IN JESUS

The entirety of the ministry of Jesus must be viewed in light of Jesus fulfilling the role of Israel. When Jesus was opening the eyes of the blind, he
was doing what Israel was called to do. Once he finished his work, he then
commissioned his followers to go to the ends of the earth and be the light
of the world.

That is why Jesus could exhort the rich young ruler to sell his land;[8]
and why the early church did so![9] It is because the fulfillment has come in
Christ and now the nations are to receive the blessings. We must no longer
be attached to the land or to one ethnicity. The nations are waiting to hear
and to see! This is what Jesus was announcing! The nations are coming in
too! Once Jesus accomplished redemption through the cross and his resurrection, it was now time to send his followers to the nations to announce
that this work is done. It is time for everyone to come to the banquet! Thus,
as Paul exhorts, "Let it be known to you that this salvation of God has been
sent to the Gentiles" (Acts 28:28).

---

8. Cf. Mark 10:17–22; Matt 19:16–22; Luke 18:18–23. Note: both Matthew and
Mark acknowledge that the man owned much "property" (Mark 10:22; Matt 19:22).

9. Cf. Acts 4:32–37; 5:1–11.

CONCLUSION

To suggest that 1948 is a fulfillment of prophecy "is to read the Old Testament as though Jesus Christ had not come into the world, and as though the New Testament had not been written, for the New Testament shows that these oracles of salvation find their fulfillment in Christ and his church."[10] The NT is clear: these promises are not still waiting to be fulfilled in the future by physical/ethnic Israelites, because they have already been fulfilled by Christ! This does not exclude modern-day Israelites from experiencing the blessings. It just means to do so they must have "the faith of our father Abraham" (Rom 4:12).[11]

10. Alastair Donaldson, "The Kingdom of God and the Land: A New Testament Fulfillment of an Old Testament Theme," in *The Gospel and the Land of Promise: Christian Approaches to the Land of the Bible* (eds. Church, Walker, Bulkeley, and Meadowcroft; Eugene, OR: Wipf and Stock, 2011) 69.

11. Nor does it justify atrocities against the Jews, which Christians have sponsored and participated in. The Bible never gives grounds for such heinous acts. God has not rejected Israel. Instead, he has fulfilled his promises to Israel. Anyone who fails to come to him in faith, whether a Jew or a Gentile, has rejected God. Our role as the children of God is to extend love to all so that God in his grace might bring all into the family of God.

Part 4

Our Responsibility in the Holy Land Today

Chapter 15

These Brothers of Mine

As he was traveling, it happened that he was approaching Damascus, and
suddenly a light from heaven flashed around him; and he fell to the ground and
heard a voice saying to him, "Saul, Saul, why are you persecuting Me?" And he
said, "Who are You, Lord?" And He said, "I am Jesus whom you are persecuting."

—ACTS 9:3–5

L et me just say it: To oppose God's people is to oppose God himself. This
assertion may at first glance appear to be an overstatement. However,
according to the Scriptures, it is unequivocally true. The fact is that one's
treatment of the people of God is indicative of one's treatment of God
himself. In addition to this, the NT also affirms that one's treatment of the
people of God forms the basis of judgment day. Though this also may appear a bit of an overstatement, this principle is found explicitly in the parable of the Sheep and the Goats in Matthew 25:31–46. The importance of
this for our perspective on matters such as Israeli-Palestinian conflict will
be addressed in the conclusion.

PAUL'S (SAUL'S) PERSECUTION OF CHRISTIANS WAS AN ATTACK ON JESUS

Perhaps the clearest indication of the fact that one's treatment of God's people is equated with one's treatment of God himself is Paul's[1] encounter with the risen Lord on the road to Damascus. According to the narrative of Acts, Paul was traveling to Damascus to have Christians who fled Jerusalem on account of his persecution extradited back to Jerusalem to face charges (Acts 9:1–2). Suddenly, he was met by the risen Christ who inquired of him, "Saul, Saul, why are you persecuting me?" (Acts 9:5). Paul then queried, "Who are You, Lord?" (Acts 9:5), to which Jesus replied, "I am Jesus whom you are persecuting" (Acts 9:5). Here Paul, thinking he was doing the will of God by persecuting Christians, is now confronted with the risen Lord. Not only does he learn that Jesus is Lord, but he also learns that it was Jesus himself whom he was persecuting.

This point is significant and cannot escape our notice; namely, that Paul learns that in his efforts to persecute Christians it was actually Jesus whom he was persecuting: "Why are you persecuting *Me*?" This must have been quite a revelation to him. Paul, a devout follower of God, was now confronted with the reality that he was in fact persecuting the very God he thought he was serving! We can only imagine what Paul must have thought at this moment!

But how could Jesus say to Paul that he was persecuting him? After all, Jesus had died and ascended to heaven. In what sense could it be possible that Paul was persecuting Jesus? The answer to this question resides in the fact that the people of God are chosen to be the means through which God builds his kingdom. It is the people of God who are carrying out the mission of God. And in doing so, they represent God and his kingdom to the world. Therefore, to persecute them is to persecute the one who sent them.

THE PARABLE OF THE SHEEP AND THE GOATS

But when the Son of Man comes in His glory, and all the angels with Him, then He will sit on His glorious throne. All the nations will be gathered before Him; and He will separate them from one another, as the shepherd separates the sheep from the goats; and He will put the sheep on His right, and the goats on the left. Then the King will say to those on His right, "Come, you who are blessed

1. He was still referred to by his Hebraic name "Saul" at this time.

of My Father, inherit the kingdom prepared for you from the foundation of the world. For I was hungry, and you gave Me *something* to eat; I was thirsty, and you gave Me *something* to drink; I was a stranger, and you invited Me in; naked, and you clothed Me; I was sick, and you visited Me; I was in prison, and you came to Me." Then the righteous will answer Him, "Lord, when did we see You hungry, and feed You, or thirsty, and give You *something* to drink? And when did we see You a stranger, and invite You in, or naked, and clothe You? When did we see You sick, or in prison, and come to You?" The King will answer and say to them, "Truly I say to you, to the extent that you did it to one of these brothers of Mine, *even the least of them*, you did it to Me." Then He will also say to those on His left, "Depart from Me, accursed ones, into the eternal fire which has been prepared for the devil and his angels; for I was hungry, and you gave Me *nothing* to eat; I was thirsty, and you gave Me nothing to drink; I was a stranger, and you did not invite Me in; naked, and you did not clothe Me; sick, and in prison, and you did not visit Me." Then they themselves also will answer, "Lord, when did we see You hungry, or thirsty, or a stranger, or naked, or sick, or in prison, and did not take care of You?" Then He will answer them, "Truly I say to you, to the extent that you did not do it to one of the least of these, you did not do it to Me." These will go away into eternal punishment, but the righteous into eternal life. (Matt 25:31–46)

This parable climaxes with "And the King will answer and say to them, 'Truly I say to you, to the extent that you did to one of the least of these brothers of mine, you did to me'" (Matt 25:40).[2] In doing so, this parable explicitly links one's treatment of "the least of these brothers of mine" to how one treats Christ. In addition to this, the parable also contends that one's treatment of such forms the basis of judgment day.[3] But who are "the least of these brothers of mine"?

2. My own translation. This translation is essentially the same as that found in all of the major English translations: The NASB, which I have used throughout this book, varies somewhat, rendering it with "one of these brothers of mine, *even* the least of them"—what my translation accomplishes is to keep the adjective "least" with the noun it is modifying ("brothers"), instead of parsing it out into a separate clause. This is important, as we will see below. And it corresponds to most of the major English translations which keep "least" with "brothers"—the ESV translates it "the least of these my brothers"; the NET translates it "the least of these brothers or sisters of mine"; the NKJV translates it "the least of these My brethren"; and the NRSV translates it "the least of these who are my members of my family."

3. It is not significant for our purposes as to whether or not the judgment depicted

It is not surprising that a number of different identifications have been offered for the "least of these brothers of mine." It is my contention that "the least of these" and "these brothers of mine" are best understood as followers of Christ.

To confirm this we must first understand the role of this parable in its immediate context and in the Gospel of Matthew as a whole. Then we must examine the use of these phrases in the Gospel of Matthew.

The Five Speeches of Matthew

First, it is widely recognized that the Gospel of Matthew contains five speeches of Jesus. R.T. France notes that that these five discourses are "widely recognized as a distinctive feature of Matthew's gospel."[4] The five speeches are found in Matthew 5–7; 10; 13; 18; and 24–25.

These five speeches are easily identified because Matthew formally marks the end of each speech by inserting the transitional phrase "And it came to pass when Jesus finished . . ." immediately after the close of each speech (cf. 7:28; 11:1; 13:53; 19:1; 26:1).[5] Since this phrase only occurs after these five extended speeches of Jesus, it is apparent that Matthew has employed it as a textual marker indicating the close of these speeches.[6]

The fifth and final speech of Jesus is often deemed the "Olivet Discourse."[7] This speech begins in either Matthew 23:2 or Matthew 24:4—though determining such is not vital to our concerns. What is important for our interest is that we may be certain that the Parable of the Sheep and the Goats (Matt 25:31–46) not only resides in this final speech, but that it serves as the conclusion of this speech.[8]

---

in Matt 25 is the final judgment or some preliminary judgment. We are only concerned to point out that the basis of judgment is one's treatment of the "least of these brothers of mine."

4. France, *Matthew*, 7.

5. Greek: *kai egeneto hote etelesen ho Iesous* (cf. 7:28; 11:1; 13:53; 19:1; 26:1).

6. Interestingly, Matthew does not provide any consistent formula marking the beginning of each of the five speeches. Consequently, the formal beginning of each speech is subject to modest debate. Nonetheless, the basic parameters of the five speeches are chs. 5–7; 10; 13; 18; and 24–25.

7. So named because beginning in 24:3 Jesus is located on the Mount of Olives.

8. This is evident from the fact that immediately following the close of this parable Matthew inserts the phrase "And it came to pass when Jesus finished . . ." (Matt 26:1). This phrase clearly marks 26:1 as the beginning of a new section and, consequently, indicates

The Four Parables of Matthew 24–25

This fifth and final sermon of Jesus in Matthew actually ends with a series of four parables,[9] with the Parable of the Sheep and the Goats being the last. The speech itself opens with the disciples questioning Jesus, "What will be the sign of your coming?" (Matt 24:3).[10] Jesus' response to this question is that he does not know: "But of that day and hour no one knows, not even the angels of heaven, nor the Son, but the Father alone" (Matt 24:36). Jesus then exhorts his disciples that since "no one knows" the "day or the hour," they are to remain "on the alert"[11] (Matt 24:43) at all times.

> Therefore *be on the alert*, for you do not know which day your Lord is coming. But be sure of this, that if the head of the house had known at what time of the night the thief was coming, he would have been on the alert and would not have allowed his house to be broken into. For this reason you also must be ready; for the Son of Man is coming at an hour when you do not think *He will*." (Matt 24:42–44)

Now, if the speech ended in Matthew 24:44, we could imagine the disciples querying as to what it might mean to "be on the alert." The speech, however, does not end here. And beginning in Matthew 24:45, Matthew inserts four parables that serve both to provide insight as to what it means to be "on the alert," as well as the consequences for those who fail to do so.

Matt 25:46 as the closing of this speech.

9. The parable of the Faithful and Wise Servant (24:45–51), the parable of the Ten Virgins (25:1–13), the parable of the Talents (25:14–30), and the parable of the Sheep and the Goats (25:31–46).

10. One could argue that the speech of Matt 23 is the formal beginning of this final speech. Matt 23 contains the words of Christ that provides the background for his declaration that Jerusalem and the temple are going to be destroyed—namely, because the people failed to repent at the coming of Christ. The "woes" of ch. 23 lead to the specific declaration that the temple will be destroyed (Matt 23:38). This leads to the questions of Matt 24. It is not pertinent to our discussion here as to whether or not these words are part of the speech of Matt 24 and 25.

11. Gk. *Gregoreite* (cf. Matt 24:43; 25:13). The general command to be watchful occurs at least seven times in Mark 13—Mark does vary the verb (unfortunately, English translations do not consistently render the same verb with the same English word): "see to it" (*blepete*: 13:5, 9, 23, 33); "stay on the alert" (*gregoreo*: 13:34, 35, 37).

Parable of the Faithful and Wise Servant

The first parable is that of the Faithful and Wise Servant (Matt 24:45–51). Contrary to many popular readings of this speech, there is nothing here that indicates the time of Jesus' return. In fact, the servant in this parable displays no concern at all with when the master is returning. Instead, the servant is only to be concerned with doing the master's will until he returns. We may surmise that the Parable of the Faithful and Wise Servant informs us that to "be on the alert" means being faithful by doing the master's will. Unfortunately, this does not provide much insight. After all, this only raises the question: what does it mean to do the master's will?

Jesus seemingly provides a measure of insight within this parable when he explains that the master's will is defined as caring for those within the master's household. In particular, the faithful servant is the one who is giving the members of the household "their food at the proper time" (Matt 24:45).

This parable highlights the consequence for failing to do so. For we are informed that the master may return unexpectedly. When he does, judgment will fall on those who fail to care for the members of the household. In fact, the master "will cut him in pieces and assign him a place with the hypocrites; in that place there will be weeping and gnashing of teeth" (Matt 24:51).

Parable of the Ten Bridesmaids and the Parable of the Talents

The Olivet Discourse continues into Matthew 25 with the Parable of the Ten Bridesmaids (Matt 25:1–13). This parable affirms the necessity of being on the alert. Again, it is stressed that the bridesmaids "do not know the day nor the hour" (Matt 25:13).

This parable is then followed by the Parable of the Talents (Matt 25:14–30). The Parable of the Talents serves to intensify the warning to those who are unfaithful. For we are told that those who are not on the alert will be "cast . . . into the outer darkness" (Matt 25:30).

Neither of these parables, however, provide any insight into what it means to "be on the alert." They do serve to intensify the warning to be prepared. Nonetheless, at this point all we know is that being "on the alert" means to give the members of the household "their food at the proper time."

Parable of the Sheep and the Goats

The Olivet Discourse then closes with the Parable of the Sheep and the Goats. This parable serves to provide the needed clarity both as to what it means to "be on the alert" and with regard to the punishment that awaits those who fail to be on the alert.[12]

In this parable, Jesus explains that at his return[13] he will separate all the nations (Matt 25:32). He will place the sheep on the right and the goats on the left (Matt 25:33). The sheep are first brought forward that they may "inherit the kingdom prepared for you from the foundation of the world" (Matt 25:34).

The key, for our interests, is that the means by which he identifies those who are the sheep and those who are the goats is how one has treated Jesus. He declares,

> I was hungry, and you gave Me *something* to eat; I was thirsty, and you gave Me *something* to drink; I was a stranger, and you invited Me in; naked, and you clothed Me; I was sick, and you visited Me; I was in prison, and you came to Me. (Matt 25:35–36)

These assertions then invoke a response by the righteous: "Then the righteous will answer Him, 'Lord, when did we see You hungry, and feed You, or thirsty, and give You *something* to drink? And when did we see You a stranger, and invite You in, or naked, and clothe You? When did we see You sick, or in prison, and come to You?'" (Matt 25:37–39). The reply is straightforward: "Truly I say to you, as long as you did to one of the least of these brothers of Mine, you did to me."[14]

Thus, Jesus exhorts his disciples that since they do not know the time of his return, they are always to "be on the alert" (Matt 24:42–44). The Parable of the Sheep and the Goats then defines being on the alert as caring for "the least of these brothers of Mine" (Matt 25:40). Furthermore, we learn that one's care for them is reflective of one's care for Jesus himself (Matt 25:40).

This, of course, raises the question "Who are the 'least of these brothers of mine'?"

---

12. Jesus also speaks more directly as to the consequences for failing to do so. They entail "eternal fire" (Matt 25:41) and "eternal punishment" (Matt 25:46).

13. The timing and nature of this return of Christ is much disputed. It is beyond our concerns however.

14. Personal translation. See n[x-ref] above.

Identifying the "Least of These Brothers of Mine" (Matt 25:40) and the "Least of These" (Matt 25:45)

Historically the identification of "the least of these brothers of Mine" (Matt 25:40) or "least of these" (Matt 25:45) has been along one of three main lines of interpretation.[15] First, some[16] suggest that they consist of all the poor and marginalized in the world. A second view[17] contends that they are the eschatological Jewish people.[18] A third position, which I will argue for, is that the "least of these brothers of mine" transcends ethnic Israelites and includes all the followers of Jesus.[19]

15. The Sheep and the Goats has been variously understood throughout the history of the church. See Gray, *Least of My Brothers*, 1989.

16. Among whom are: Hunter, *Interpreting the Parables*; Tasker, *Gospel according to Matthew*; Henry, *Personal Christian Ethics*, 229f.; Cox, "Eschatology of the Gospels," 222.

17. This view is held almost exclusively by dispensationalist writers. Ladd notes that he had found only one non-dispensational writer who espoused this view—referring to J. A. Findlay (Ladd, *Parables of Sheep and Goats*, 195).

18. The variations within this view relate to whether or not one should identify one particular faction of the Jewish people (typically it is proposed that this is some sort of eschatological Jewish people who live during the tribulation). For many dispensationalist writers the judgment of the sheep and the goats is determinative for which of the Gentile nations will enter the millennial kingdom. One of the significant difficulties with the dispensationalist reading here is that this passage is simply read in light of the assumptions of the entire dispensationalist schema. This schema, however, must be assumed. Nowhere in this passage do we have even an allusion to the rapture, the eschatological conversion of Jews, the dispensational notion of a seven year tribulation, or a millennial kingdom. Ladd notes, "I must say here that this parable and its exegesis was one of the factors that shook my faith in the dispensationalist system." Ladd cites Walvoord, "a correct exegesis of this passage demands first of all strict adherence to the exact wording of this revelation." Ladd then concludes, "If this norm is followed strictly, however, one must conclude that the righteous do not enter a millenial kingdom but rather enter directly into eternal life. . . . If this parable is meant to be a program of the end, I must conclude that there is no room for a millenial kingdom." Ladd, *Parables of Sheep and Goats*, 196.

19. I say "transcends ethnic Israelites" because the nature of the people of God since Christ is that they are composed of men and women from all nations and this certainly includes Israelites. That is, this is not a debate of Jews versus Christians—as is too often proposed. Instead, it is a debate about "promise and fulfillment," or "just promise." The "just promise" view suggests that it refers only to the physical descendants of Abraham. The "promise and fulfillment" view suggests that it now includes all the nations, which themselves arose from OT Israel and includes Israelites.

The variations within this latter viewpoint relate to whether or not these are specific followers of Jesus (such as the apostles) or if they represent all of the followers of Jesus in history. One could attempt to argue that "these brothers of mine" refers exclusively to the apostles. After all, the context of this sermon relates directly to their apostolic

This view is based on the fact that both "these brothers of mine" and the adjective "least" are used unambiguously in the Gospel of Matthew for the followers of Christ.[20]

"Brothers of Mine" in Matthew

The word "brother" (Gk. *adelphos*) occurs thirty-nine times in Matthew. In many instances it refers to someone as the direct biological brother of someone else,[21] or in a more generic sense of someone who is either biologically or ethnically related.[22] None of these uses of "brother," however, provide any insight into the meaning of Matthew 25:40.

This points us to a third use of "brother" in Matthew's gospel—namely, that it refers to those who follow Christ. This is supported by the fact that "brother" in Matthew 25:40 is used in conjunction with the pronoun "mine." Ladd affirms, "There is no precedent in Matthew or in the teaching of Jesus to identify Jesus' brethren as his Jewish kinsman. . . . Jesus never speaks of the Jews as *his* brethren, whereas he does speak of his disciples as his brethren (Matt 12:46–50)."[23]

The use of "brother" to refer to the followers of Christ is also supported by the explicit declaration in Matthew 12. Matthew notes that Jesus asks,

> "Who is My mother and who are My brothers?" And stretching out His hand toward His disciples, He said, "Behold My mother and My brothers! For whoever does the will of My Father who is in heaven, he is My brother and sister and mother." (Matt 12:48–50)

For, Jesus and his first-century world this was a radical redefinition of family. No longer are family relations to be determined by ethnicity or even familial relations.[24]

---

mission. This is the approach of J. Ramsey Michaels. See Michaels, "Apostolic Hardships and Righteous Gentiles," 27–38. That the mission to which the apostles are sent applies universally to the people of God strongly suggests that "these brothers of mine" likewise extends to all of the people of God.

20. Matt 12:48, 49, and 50; cf. also 5:22–24, 47; 7:3–5; 18:15, 21, 35; 23:8; 28:10.

21. See Matt 1:2, 11; 4:18 (2x), 21 (2x); 10:2 (2x), 21 (2x); 12:46, 47; 13:55; 14:3; 17:1; 19:29; 20:24; 22:24 (2x), 25 (2x).

22. Matt 5:22 (2x), 23, 24, 47; 7:3, 4, 5; 18:15 (2x), 21, 35.

23. Ladd, *Parables of Sheep and Goats*, 196.

24. Stassen affirms, "In the New Testament, 'brother' usually means fellow community

This redefined sense of the followers of Christ as his brothers is also found in Matthew 28:10: "Then Jesus said to them, 'Do not be afraid; go and take word to My brethren to leave for Galilee, and there they will see Me.'"

Therefore, the reference to the sheep as Jesus' "brothers" indicates that he is referring to his followers.

"Least" and "Little Ones" in Matthew

Jesus also defines the sheep as "the least of these." The use of the superlative adjective "least" in Matthew 25:40, 45[25] with the expression "little ones" (*mikron*) in Matthew 10:42; 18:6, 10, and 14,[26] also supports the identification of the sheep as followers of Christ.

That the "little ones" are followers of Christ is apparent from the fact that Jesus identifies them as "you" in reference to his disciples in Matthew 10:40.[27] Jesus also describes the "little ones" in Matthew 18:5 as those "who believe in Me."[28] In addition, as already noted, the "little ones" in Matthew 18 are closely linked with "brothers"—whom we have already noted are identified as the followers of Jesus—in Matthew 12:50.[29]

In addition to this, there are strong indications that the "little ones" of Matthew 10 and 18 are to be identified with the "least of these" in Matthew 25:45.[30] First, the connection between the "least" in Matthew 25 and the "little ones" of Matthew 10 and Matthew 18 is suggested by the contextual similarities that link the three passages. For Matthew 10, 18, and 25 all

---

member, fellow follower of Jesus." Stassen, *Living Sermon*, 154.

25. The phrase in Matt 25:40, "least of these," functions adjectively to provide a further description of "My brothers."

26. Ladd contends, "In Jesus' teaching, 'the little ones' becomes a synonym for his disciples." He further notes, "In Matthew 25:40, the word translated 'least' serves as the superlative form of *mikros*." Ladd, "Parable of Sheep and Goats," 198. See also Hagner, *Matthew 14–28*, 745.

27. That the disciples are addressed is clear from the opening of Jesus' address in Matt 10:5: "These twelve Jesus sent out after instructing them."

28. The whole of Matt 18:6 states, "But whoever causes one of these little ones who believe in Me to stumble, it would be better for him to have a heavy millstone hung around his neck, and to be drowned in the depth of the sea."

29. They are declared to be those "who do the will of My Father."

30. Hagner affirms, "The true counterpart to the phrase 'one of these least' is found in Matthew's distinctive 'the little ones.'" Hagner, *Matthew 14–28*, 745.

indicate that how one treats the "little ones" or "the least of them" is how one treats Jesus. In Matthew 10:40, Jesus notes that "he who receives you receives Me." Matthew 25:40 similarly notes: "Truly I say to you, as long as you did to one of the least of these brothers of mine, you did to me." Finally, Matthew 18 states the same with regard to the "little ones" (cf. 18:6, 10, 14): "whoever receives one such child in My name receives Me" (Matt 18:5). Therefore, in each passage we find the principle that one's treatment of the "least of these" and the "little ones" is tantamount to one's treatment of Jesus.[31]

Second, both the "little ones" (Matt 18:6, 10, and 14) and the "least of these" (Matt 25:40, 45) are equated with "brother." In Matthew 18:14–15, Jesus states, "So it is not *the* will of your Father who is in heaven that one of these little ones perish. If your brother sins, go and show him his fault in private; if he listens to you, you have won your brother." The association of "brother" with both "least" (Matt 25:40) and "little ones" (Matt 18:14) strongly ties these passages.

Third, "these little ones" (Matt 10:42) and the "least of these brothers of mine" (Matt 25:40) are linked by the reference to the giving of a drink to each. In Matthew 10:42, Jesus states, "Whoever in the name of a disciple gives to one of these little ones even a cup of cold water to drink." In the same way, in Matthew 25:37 Jesus explains that by giving a drink to one of "the least of them" one has given a drink to him (Matt 27:40).[32]

Fourth, both Matthew 10 and Matthew 25 convey a strong sense of blessing or judgment on the one who provides or withholds for the "little ones" or the "least of these." In Matthew 10:40–42, the promise of blessing for one who provides for the "little ones" means that one will "certainly not lose his reward."[33] In Matthew 25:31–46, those who provide for "these brothers of Mine, even the least of these" are promised that they will "inherit the kingdom" (Matt 25:34).

From this it is clear that "the least of these brothers of mine" in the Gospel of Matthew refers to the followers of Jesus.

---

31. Hagner concludes, "Jesus thus identified himself fully with his disciples." Hagner, *Matthew 14–28*, 744.

32. Hagner, *Matthew 14–28*, 745.

33. My translation. The use of "certainly" here is quite emphatic in the Greek (which employs the emphatic double negative *ou me*) and worthy of being noted in translation—as in the NIV. Cf. the NLT use of "surely"; the ESV and NKJV "by no means"; and the NET Bible's "he will never."

CONCLUSION

In light of the Parable of the Sheep and the Goats, we may affirm that to "be on the alert" is defined by Jesus as providing those within the master's household with their food. Are they feeding, clothing, visiting in prison, and caring for God's people—who are defined as the "the least of these brothers of Mine" (Matt 25:40)? Therefore, how one treats the followers of Jesus is how one treats Jesus.[34] Ladd affirms, "The good deeds done to Jesus' brethren are not mere works of morality and decency. They show how they stood toward the kingdom of God. Were they on the side of the kingdom or against it?"[35]

This conclusion in no way mitigates our responsibility to love and care for all people. Morris affirms that even though "the least of these" refers to Christians, this "does not give the follower of Jesus license to do good deeds to fellow Christians but none to outsiders."[36]

Instead this simply affirms that our love and concern for all people must begin with our love and concern for one another: just as a father's responsibility to care for his household takes precedent over his concern for others.

34. This is further supported by the opening reference in the Parable of the Sheep and the Goats to the "Son of Man" (Matt 25:31). For the Son of Man in Dan 7:13–14 is the representative "of the holy people of God." See France, *Matthew*, 965.

35. Ladd, "Parables of Sheep and Goats," 197.

36. Morris, *Matthew*, 639.

Chapter 16

Must We Bless Israel
to Be Blessed by God?[1]

Acommon assumption among Christian Zionists is the refrain that we must bless Israel. Sandra Teplinsky asserts, "Do you want more of the Blesser? If so, you want to bless Israel."[2] The response here is quite simple.

First, the people of God should never support any nation—or even any person for that matter—unquestioningly. Even in the OT God did not endorse the actions of the nation of Israel at all times. The prophets were clear: election alone was not sufficient. Thus, Amos says, "You only have I chosen among all the families of the earth; Therefore, I will punish you for all your iniquities" (Amos 3:2). The people of God must do justice (Mic 6:8). If they failed to do justice, they were subject to God's judgment.

Furthermore, the Scriptures are clear that covenant faithfulness is a prerequisite for covenant blessing.

1. Now in what follows, I am in no way disparaging the Jewish people or the nation of Israel. My point here is that the blessings of the covenant come to those who are faithful to the covenant: that includes Jews and Gentiles who believe in Jesus. But it does not apply to any nation exclusively. The people of God are composed of people from many nations. We are, however, called to love everyone. We are to seek peace and justice for everyone—regardless of their race, gender, or socioeconomic status. We love Israelis and Palestinians.

2. Teplinsky, *Why Care about Israel?*, 37. Interestingly, Teplinsky also admits, "Those who bless the Church are blessed, those who curse the Church are cursed, and all the families of the earth are blessed through the Church" (37).

> But if you do not obey Me and do not carry out all these com-
> mandments, if, instead, you reject My statutes, and if your soul
> abhors My ordinances so as not to carry out all My command-
> ments, *and* so break My covenant, I, in turn, will do this to you: I
> will appoint over you a sudden terror, consumption and fever that
> shall waste away the eyes and cause the soul to pine away; also,
> you shall sow your seed uselessly, for your enemies shall eat it up.
> And I will set My face against you so that you shall be struck down
> before your enemies; and those who hate you shall rule over you,
> and you shall flee when no one is pursuing you. If also after these
> things, you do not obey Me, then I will punish you seven times
> more for your sins. (Lev 26:14–18)

The book of Leviticus goes on to say (as does Deuteronomy, which
forms the basis for the books of Joshua-Kings) that the land will "spew"
them out if they are unfaithful (Lev 18:28; 20:22).

In fact, throughout the OT, the Israelites who were not obedient to
God's law were not blessed. For example, during the exodus any Israelite
who failed to put blood on their doorposts also lost their firstborn. Also,
the unfaithful Israelites who came out of Egypt were not permitted to enter
the Promise Land. They instead died in the wilderness.

Additionally, even if we supposed that the physical descendants of
Abraham were to be restored to the land, as Christian Zionists claim—and
this supposedly in accord with the promises of the OT—we must also recognize that they are still to be held to standards of justice. This is unquestioningly the message of the prophets:

> Is this not the fast which I choose, to loosen the bonds of wicked-
> ness, to undo the bands of the yoke, and to let the oppressed go
> free, and break every yoke? Is it not to divide your bread with the
> hungry, and bring the homeless poor into the house; when you see
> the naked, to cover him; and not to hide yourself from your own
> flesh?" (Isa 58:6–7)

The point here is that we must not assume that any people are blessed
by God regardless of their actions.

Furthermore, we have seen that even in the OT the people of God were
never restricted to a nation, or just the physical descendants of Abraham.
For one, the people of God in the OT included Ruth, Rahab, and others
who were not direct descendants of Abraham, Isaac, and Jacob. In addition, Jesus understood that Abraham's offspring were those who had the
faith of Abraham. Thus, John records Jesus' rebuke of the Pharisees: "They

answered and said to Him, 'Abraham is our father.' Jesus said to them, 'If you are Abraham's children, do the deeds of Abraham'" (John 8:39).

JESUS AND HIS FOLLOWERS ARE THE PEOPLE OF GOD

In addition to all this we have seen throughout this book that the promises to Abraham and Israel regarding family are fulfilled in Jesus and the NT people of God, and that the climax of their fulfillment is in the New Jerusalem. What then does this mean for the promise of blessing to those who bless the people of God?

The answer to this is straightforward. If the people of God are Jesus and his followers, then it stands to reason that any promise of blessing or curse is dependent on how one treats them. That is, the promise of blessing and cursing is not dependent upon how one treats the modern nation of Israel, but how one treats the people of God—i.e., Jesus and those who have faith in him. We have seen that the principle is clear: how one treats God's people is how one treats God himself.

In the NT the people of God are clearly defined as: "whoever does the will of God, he is My brother and sister and mother" (Mark 3:35). Jesus' redefinition of family is vital to the NT. This is not to say that the NT changes the definition of the people of God in a way that eliminates the Jewish people. The NT redefinition of the people of God is a broadening of the people of God to include Gentiles. It is not true, then, to say that in the OT the people of God were defined along the physical lines of Abraham's descendants; while in the NT they are defined spiritually as those who believe in Jesus. We might say that the people of God were always defined by those who had the faith of Abraham. In the NT, we see that this comes to include Gentiles more programmatically.

It is faith that makes a person a child of Abraham in God's eyes. This is not a NT thing as though God suddenly changed the rules. Paul affirms, referring to Abraham, "so that he might be the father of all who believe without being circumcised. . . . For this reason *it is* by faith, in order that *it may be* in accordance with grace, so that the promise will be guaranteed to all the descendants, not only to those who are of the Law [Jews], but also to those who are of the faith of Abraham [Gentiles], who is the father of us all [Jews and Gentiles]" (Rom 4:11, 16).

CONCLUSION

Therefore, if we want to invoke the promise of blessing in Genesis 12:1–3, we must understand two points. First, the promise of blessings and curses applies to those who bless or curse God's people. God's people are defined as those who do the will of God. This has always been the case, though it is true that in the OT era the people of God were primarily composed of Israelites. The NT does not change this to suddenly mean that Jews are no longer part of the people of God, but others are. Instead, the NT simply notes that those who do the will of God now include Gentiles. Second, the people of God today are not restricted to a nation[3] but are comprised of people from every nation.[4]

To suggest that we should unquestioningly support the state of Israel in the present conflict in the Holy Land is gravely mistaken. We should not support any nation to the exclusion of, or over against, another nation. We must support God's people who presently dwell in most nations of the world. Furthermore, we must support justice and peace for the sake of all. This is what Christian love looks like.

3. Though it is correct to say that the people of God were a nation in the OT era, we must clarify—namely, that this statement is only a general statement. That is, not everyone in the nation was a member of the people of God, since not everyone had the faith of Abraham.

4. Though Gen 12:1–3 may not be completely fulfilled in the present, the point still stands that today God's people are from many nations.

Part 5

Conclusion

Chapter 17

What Does This All Mean
for the Church Today?

Sometimes matters of theological disputes within Christianity have few
social, political, or even economic implications. Do we baptize infants
or wait until they become old enough to make a decision for themselves?
One person may say baptize them, while another says to wait. Sure, the
implications may be significant as far as God is concerned; and I do not
intend to disparage the theological significance of such issues. But when
it comes to the day-to-day affairs of life on this earth there is little impact.

In many ways, I wish that this book were just another theological
treatise that debated the finer points of Christian theology—that I was just
another contributor to a theological issue. Unfortunately, the theological
positions relating to the temple, the people of God, and the land have had
far ranging effects.

Why does it matter what we believe about the temple, the people, and
the land? It matters for a number of reasons. One of these is that evangelical
Christianity has allowed the popular convictions of Christian Zionism to
dramatically affect our view of what is happening in the Holy Land. Unfortunately, life in the Holy Land is difficult for Jews, Muslims, and Christians.[1]
The present conflict has, unfortunately, been fostered in large part because

---

1. This book has done little to address these issues. See below, or consult the bibliography for resources that will help us see what life on the ground in the Holy Land is
really like for Christian, Jews, and Muslims.

of evangelical Christians and their theological convictions of Christian Zionism. This book is intended to bring awareness that our theological convictions on such matters are not a set of isolated ramblings with little to no effect on the world. Quite the contrary. The effects are significant.

THE GOSPEL AND THE KINGDOM ARE AT STAKE

For one, the gospel is at stake. Jesus commanded us to be peacemakers. When we advocate for war, or at the least when we do not advocate for peace, we are failing to live up to the standards of the gospel. One of the greatest hindrances to our successful witness to the world is the attitude of many evangelicals towards peace in the Middle East and towards Middle Easterners in particular. We have not only failed to model Jesus to the world, we have failed to heed the cries of our own brothers and sisters in Christ, and we have been a poor witness to the world.

If the Parable of the Sheep and the Goats means what I think it means, then we must advocate for the people in the Holy Land—at least for the sake of our Christian brothers and sisters.

What I attempted to do in the first two sections of this book was to address the theological issues that cause many evangelicals to adopt a stance that is decidedly one-sided (most commonly pro-Israel). A proper response to the theological section of this book is not to simply revert to the other side and become pro-Palestinian. If anything, I hope to have simply dismissed the theological assertions that force Christians to one side or the other. If we adopt one side, it should be the side of the kingdom of God. This would force us to begin by advocating for the Christian community. It would also mean that we must advocate for peace, justice, and the well-being of all people. This means that we are on every side.

Though I will provide below a few concrete steps whereby we might become engaged, I would like to suggest that we start with the well-being of our brothers and sisters in Christ—the "least of these my brothers." The reality is that the conflict in Israel/Palestine has serious ramifications for "these brothers of mine"—whether they are Israeli or Palestinian Christians. Forget, for a moment, about whether all this is the fulfillment of prophecy, and the questions about the land and the restoration of Israel. What about the people of God? Are they not the "least of these brothers of mine"?

Just as God heard the cries of his people in Exodus 2 and responded by calling Moses to rescue them, so also, God hears the cries of his people and responds by calling his people to rescue them. Thus, today, as when God called Moses in Egypt thousands of years ago, redemption begins with the calling of the people of God.

WHERE DO WE GO FROM HERE?

The purpose of this book has been to provide a biblical understanding of temple, people, and land in Scripture, as well as a theological response to Christian Zionism. However, I do not want to simply end there. I believe that this response is vital for several reasons. First, I believe that Christian Zionism is a misreading of Scripture. In my previous book, *Understanding Eschatology: Why it Matters*, I argued that a proper understanding of Jesus as the fulfillment of Scripture is essential because the mission which Jesus accomplished is the very mission that we are called to carry out.

In this book I have taken this understanding one step further—namely, that the work of Christ must be understood in terms of his fulfilling the mission and role of Israel. As "fellow heirs" with Christ (Rom 8:17), we too must understand our mission in terms of the call of Israel. That call was to be a "light to the nations" (Isa 42:6; cf. 49:6). But we cannot be a light to the nations when we advocate for war in the Middle East as a result of some theological convictions about the end-times. For in doing so we are not exemplifying the love of Christ and the necessity of being bearers of peace.

Second, many in the Western Christian church[2] have espoused Christian Zionist ideology and have actively supported the state of Israel over against the Palestinians. This is not to say that we cannot support the state of Israel. I am, however, suggesting that we must be cautious of favoring one state (often Israel, though some are advocating for Palestine over-against Israel) exclusively. This is especially problematic when others are suffering as a result of our exclusive support of Israel or Palestine; some of those who are suffering are our Christian brothers and sisters.

Third, we have a biblical responsibility to be engaged in caring for our brothers and sisters in Christ. This is not some secondary command whereby it might be a good idea if we were able to do it. Instead, this command is vital to the very nature of being a follower of Christ: "By this all men will know that you are My disciples, if you have love for one another" (John 13:35).

2. As a result of the Western church's influence, the ideas of Christian Zionism are indeed spreading to the global church.

WHAT DO WE DO NOW?

We need to get involved. But what does involvement look like? There are plenty of people that are far more astute at answering questions pertaining to the social, political, and international affairs than me. Thus, I will attempt to point you in what I think are some of the proper directions for Western evangelical Christians.

First, get informed. I am firmly convinced that awareness is the number one factor needed to change the situation.[3] Getting informed can take a lot of different forms. To begin with I would suggest that you personally get to know some people in your local areas that are Jewish and Palestinian Christians. You will not be disappointed. You might be stretched and challenged but you will not be disappointed. They are wonderful people. As you do so, you might also get to know others who are Jewish or Arab—whether they are Christians or not. Learn their stories. Find out who they are. Where they have come from. Ask them how you can better understand their culture and way of life. And let them know that you care and why you care.

Next, I would recommend that you connect with people who live in the land. Get in touch with Israeli and Palestinian Christians in the Holy Land. One of my favorite people is Daoud Nassar. I can honestly say that in all my travels and teaching I do not believe that I have met a man and a family that exemplifies the love of Christ more than Daoud and his family. Visit his website (http://www.tentofnations.org) to learn more of his life, struggles, and witness in the land. There is a wonderful video that captures Daoud's story available at http://vimeo.com/29677206. Another wonderful ministry in the Holy Land is that of Musalaha (http://www.musalaha.org). Musalaha, Arabic for "reconciliation," is a ministry that aims to connect Israeli and Palestinian Christians in order to bring reconciliation among them.

Also, you can get informed by means of a wealth of fantastic resources. In the bibliography I have listed many resources for you to begin your journey—books, videos, and websites. One of the best places to start is *Blood*

---

3. Even if a political solution comes about by political negotiations, in order for this solution to have any lasting effect, it must be met with a will to succeed. This will to succeed will require evangelical Christians to support the peace process. I fear that too many evangelicals will lash out at Secretary Kerry, President Obama, and any others for their efforts to secure peace, because it will be thought that they have forced God's chosen people (modern-day Israel) to compromise.

Brothers by Elias Chacour. There are a number of quality films being produced by Just Vision (http://www.justvision.org), which is an international organization that uses film and media to work towards a just peace.

After getting informed you can take a visit to the land. But do not simply go to see the sites where Jesus walked. Go and see the "living stones"—the Christians who live and work in the land. Anytime one travels to another land, the most enriching thing one can do is to meet the locals. Meeting the locals in the Holy Land is especially rewarding! One of the best ways to accomplish this type of trip is to work with the Telos Group (http://www.telosgroup.org/). A trip with the Telos group will enable you to experience the places that Jesus walked and to meet leaders and locals among the Israelis and Palestinians. There is no better way to tour the Holy Land. World Vision also offers some tours that help you connect with the people of the land.

Third, you can get active. Mind you that this is definitely third on the list. I strongly urge you not to become too zealous for the cause until you have become more informed. A little knowledge and a lot of zeal is a dangerous mix and may likely do more harm than good. So prayerfully take the time to get informed and to meet the people—both those in your own community and those in the Holy Land. As you do so, you will begin to learn more as to what getting involved in your local community might look like.

Involvement can mean so many things. It can mean prayer. It can mean giving to ministries that are already working in the land—including the Tent of Nations, Musalaha, World Vision (http://www.worldvision.org; which has child sponsorships and other endeavors in the Holy Land), Jews for Jesus (http://www.jewsforjesus.org; who are active in Israel), and Holy Land trust (http://www.holylandt rust.org; an organization that endeavors to empower the people of the Holy Land to overcome their struggles and end oppression).

In the end, we have a job to do. The mission of the kingdom of God includes being peacemakers. Christ is the temple. We too, by means of the Spirit's dwelling within us, are the temple of God. The promises of family and land to Abraham are fulfilled in Christ. Now, God desires to bless all mankind and the entirety of the earth. We, as the ambassadors of Christ, are called to be agents of God's restoration. This begins when we are advocates for peace.

IN THE END

Many might still ask: "Why should I care about what happens in Israel and Palestine?" The fact is that we must care. And we must alert the church, especially in the West, that we must care. Too much is at stake. We have Christian brothers and sisters throughout the Middle East in general and in the Holy Land in particular. Unfortunately, they have been directly impacted by our theological opinions. As a result, the church cannot be silent. It must not be silent.

Our brothers and sisters in Christ are crying out. Jesus is crying out. We must respond!

Bibliography

RECOMMENDED RESOURCES

An annotated list of resources: Though there are many wonderful resources available that discuss the theology and the human rights issues, I have chosen to keep this resource list moderately sparse and to restrict it to materials that I am personally most familiar with. I strongly recommend that everyone start their journey by reading Elias Chacour's *Blood Brothers*. From there I would encourage everyone to read Salim Munayer and Lisa Loden's *The Land Cries Out* in order to understand the issue from both a Jewish and a Palestinian perspective. One of the best resources that provides a good introduction to the whole of the issues is Gary Burge's *Whose Land? Whose Promise?* The many videos available provide an excellent way to learn and understand without the encumbrance of reading a whole book. Always read and watch with caution and an open mind. We must learn to see everyone in this conflict and human beings who deserve the peace, love, and hope.

Books

Awad, Alex. *Palestinian Memories: The Story of a Palestinian Mother and Her People.* Bethlehem: Bethlehem Bible College, 2008. Awad recounts his own story and how his mother raised seven children after his father was killed in 1948.

Barker, Margaret. *On Earth as It Is in Heaven.* Sheffield: Sheffield Pheonix, 2009.

Beale, G. K. *A New Testament Biblical Theology.* Grand Rapids: Baker Academic, 2011.

———. *The Temple and the Church's Mission.* Downers Grove: InterVarsity, 2004.

Beale, G. K., and D. A. Carson, eds. *Commentary on the New Testament Use of the Old Testament.* Grand Rapids: Baker, 2007.

Bibliography

Boyd, Gregory A., and Paul R Eddy. *Across the Spectrum: Understanding Issues in Evangelical Theology.* Grand Rapids: Baker, 2002.

Brueggemann, Walter. *The Land: Place as Gift, Promise, and Challenge in Biblical Faith.* Philadelphia: Fortress, 1976.

Burge, Gary. *Jesus and the Land.* Grand Rapids: Baker, 2010. Excellent work on understanding the issue of the Land in the Bible.

———. *Whose Land? Whose Promise?* Cleveland: Pilgrim, 2003. Excellent work—perhaps the best read for understanding the conflict as a whole.

Caird, G. B. *The Language and Imagery of the Bible.* Philadelphia: Westminster, 1980.

Chacour, Elias. *Blood Brothers.* Old Tappan, NJ: Revell, 1984. Must read.

———. *Faith Beyond Despair: Building Hope in the Holy Land.* Atlanta: Canterbury, 2008.

———. *We Belong to the Land: The Story of a Palestinian Israeli Who Lives for Peace and Reconciliation.* New York: Harper & Row, 1990.

Chapman, Colin. *Whose Promised Land?* Grand Rapids: Baker, 2002.

Church, Peter, et al., eds. *The Gospel and the Land of Promise.* Eugene, OR: Wipf & Stock, 2011. Very good theological work.

Clowney, Edmund. "The Final Temple." *Westminster Theological Journal* 35 (1973) 156–89.

Dalrymple, Rob. *Understanding Eschatology: Why It Matters!* Eugene, OR: Wipf & Stock, 2013. Provides a framework to begin to look at the theological issues that often cloud evangelical perceptions of the issue.

Davies, W. D. *The Gospel and the Land.* Berkeley: University of California Press, 1974.

Dumbrell, William J. *The End of the Beginning: Revelation 21–22 and the Old Testament.* Homebush West, Australia: Lancer, 1985.

Epp, F. H. *Whose Land Is Palestine?* Grand Rapids: Eerdmans, 1970.

Guthrie, Donald. *New Testament Theology.* Leicester: InterVarsity, 1981.

Hays, J. Daniel. *The Message of the Prophets.* Grand Rapids: Zondervan, 2010.

Hays, J. Daniel, et al. *Dictionary of Biblical Prophecy and End Times.* Grand Rapids: Zondervan, 2007.

Johnston, Philip, and Peter Walker. *The Land of Promise.* Downers Grove: InterVarsity, 2000. Very good theological work.

Ladd, George Eldon. *A Theology of the New Testament.* Grand Rapids: Eerdmans, 1974.

Loden, Lisa, et al. *The Bible and the Land: An Encounter.* Jerusalem: Musalaha, 2000.

Mitri, Raheb. *I Am a Palestinian Christian*: Minneapolis: Fortress, 1995. Pastor from Bethlehem—very good.

Motyer, Stephen. *Israel in the Plan of God.* Leicester: InterVarsity, 1989.

Munayer, Salim J., and Lisa Loden, eds. *The Land Cries Out.* Eugene, OR: Cascade, 2012. Very good theological work with both Jewish and Palestinian writers.

Ridderbos, Herman. *The Coming of the Kingdom.* Translated by H. de Jongste. Edited by Raymond O. Zorn. Philadelphia: P & R, 1962.

Schmitt, John W., and J. Carl Laney. *Messiah's Coming Temple.* Grand Rapids: Kregel, 1997.

Schnabel, Eckhard. *40 Questions about the End Times.* Grand Rapids: Kregel, 2011.

Schreiner, Thomas. *New Testament Theology: Magnifying God in Christ.* Grand Rapids: Baker, 2008.

Vlach, Michael J. *Has the Church Replaced Israel?* Nashville: Broadman & Holman, 2010.

Walker, Peter. *Jerusalem Past and Present in the Purposes of God.* Cambridge: Tyndale, 1992. Rev. ed., Grand Rapids: Baker, 1994.

———. *Jesus and the Holy City: New Testament Perspectives on Jerusalem*. Grand Rapids: Eerdmans, 1996. Excellent theological work.

Movies and DVDs

Budrus. An excellent documentary that details the nonviolent reaction of the citizens of Budrus and their efforts to alter the course of the separation barrier that threatened to cut off much of their olive groves and city.

Encounter Point. Tells the story of an Israeli settler, a Palestinian, a bereaved Israeli mother, and a Palestinian bereaved brother who risk it all to bring an end to the conflict.

Little Town of Bethlehem. A fantastic documentary that follows three young men (a Jew, a Muslim, and a Christian) and their efforts to bring peace.

Miral. The story of a Palestinian girl who grows up in the midst of the Israeli-Palestinian conflict.

Steadfast Hope. A booklet and DVD produced by the Palestine Israel Network of the Episcopal Peace Fellowship.

5 Broken Cameras. A documentary that records the nonviolent struggles of Bil'in. The film was shot almost entirely by Palestinian farmer Emad Burnat, who bought his first camera in 2005 to record the birth of his youngest son.

Websites: General

http://determinetruth.com. This is my personal website related to understanding eschatology, biblical interpretation, understanding the OT in light of the NT, Israel/Palestine, Christianity in the Middle East.

http://www.musalaha.org. Salim Munayer's ministry that works to bring reconciliation among Christians in Israel and Palestine.

http://www.dci-palestine.org. An international organization fighting for the rights of Palestinian children.

http://www.justvision.org. An international organization that used film and media to work towards a just peace. Several of their videos are listed below.

http://www.ispeacepossible.com. Superb site that gives detailed presentations on what is needed for peace to happen in the Holy Land.

Israeli Peace and Human Rights Groups

www.icahd.org. Israeli Committee Against House Demolition, a nonviolent, direct-action group originally established to oppose and resist Israeli demolition of Palestinian houses in the occupied territory.

www.btselem.org. B'tselem, an Israeli organization concerned with the abuse of Palestinian human rights in the occupied territory.

Alternative Media Resources

http://www.haaretz.com. *Ha'aretz*, an Israeli daily newspaper.

http://english.aljazeera.net. English *Aljazeera*, the world's first global English language news channel to be headquartered in the Middle East.

WORKS CITED

These works were cited in the body of this book and are in addition to those works in the recommended resource list.

Beale, G. K. *The Book of Revelation: A Commentary on the Greek Text*. New International Greek Testament Commentary. Grand Rapids: Eerdmans, 1999.

Baker, D. L. *Two Testaments, One Bible: A Study of Some Modern Solutions to the Theological Problem of the Relationship between the Old and New Testaments*. Downers Grove: InterVarsity, 1976.

Benware, Paul. *Understanding End Times Prophecy: A Comprehensive Approach*. Chicago: Moody, 2006.

Blaising, Craig A., and Darrell L. Bock, eds. *Dispensationalism, Israel and the Church*. Grand Rapids: Zondervan, 1992.

Bock, Darrell L. "The Reign of the Lord Christ." In Blaising and Bock, *Dispensationalism, Israel and the Church*, 37–67.

Cox, Steven. "The Eschatology of the Gospels." Chapter 11 in *The Return of Christ: A Premillennial Perspective*, edited by David L. Allen and Steve W. Lemke. Broadman & Holman, 2011.

Cragg, Kenneth. *The Arab Christian: A History in the Middle East*. Louisville: John Knox, 1991.

Dalrymple, Rob. *Revelation and the Two Witnesses*. Eugene, OR: Wipf & Stock, 2011.

———. "These Are the Ones." *Biblica* 86 (2005) 396–406.

Diprose, Ronald E. *Israel and the Church: The Origins and Effects of Replacement Theology*. Waynesboro, GA: Authentic Media, 2004.

Feinberg, J. S., ed. *Continuity and Discontinuity: Perspectives on the Relationship between the Old and New Testaments*. Wheaton, IL: Crossway, 1988.

Bibliography

France, R. T. *The Gospel of Matthew*. New International Commentary on the New Testament. Grand Rapids: Eerdmans, 2007.

———. "Old Testament Prophecy and the Future of Israel." *Tyndale Bulletin* 26 (1975) 53–78.

Gray, Sherman W. *The Least of My Brothers: Matthew 25:31–46; A History of Interpretation*. SBL Dissertation Series 114. Atlanta: Scholars, 1989.

Gundry, Robert. "In My Father's House Are Many Monai." *Zeitschrift für die neutestamentliche Wissenschaft und die Kunde der älteren Kirche* 58 (1967) 68–72.

Hagner, Donald Alfred. *Matthew 14–28*. Word Biblical Commentary 33b. Dallas: Word, 1995.

Henry, Carl F. H. *Personal Christian Ethics*. Grand Rapids: Eerdmans, 1957.

Horner, Barry E. *Future Israel: Why Christian Anti-Judaism Must Be Challenged*. NACSBT. Nashville: Broadman & Holman, 2007.

House, H. Wayne, ed. *Israel, the Land and the People: An Evangelical Affirmation of God's Promises*. Grand Rapids: Kregel, 1998.

Hunter, A. M. *Interpreting the Parables*. London: SCM, 1960.

Jobes, Karen. *1 Peter*. Baker Exegetical Commentary on the New Testament. Grand Rapids: Baker Academic, 2005.

Ladd, George E. "The Parable of the Sheep and the Goats in Recent Interpretation." In *New Dimensions in New Testament Study*, edited by Richard N. Longenecker and Merrill C. Tenney, 191–96. Grand Rapids: Zondervan, 1974.

Michaels, J. Ramsey. "Apostolic Hardships and Righteous Gentiles." *JBL* 84 (1965) 27–38.

Morris, Leon. *The Gospel according to Matthew*. Pillar New Testament Commentary. Grand Rapids: Eerdmans, 1992.

Pawson, David. *Defending Christian Zionism*. Travelers Rest, SC: True Potential, 2008.

Perrin, Nicholas. *Jesus the Temple*. Grand Rapids: Baker Academic, 2010.

Poythress, Vern S. *Understanding Dispensationalists*. Grand Rapids: Academie, 1987.

Pratt, Richard. "To the Jew First: A Reformed Perspective." Chapter 9 in *To the Jew First: The Case for Jewish Evangelism in Scripture and History*, edited by Darrell L. Bock and Mitch Glaser. Grand Rapids: Kregel, 2008.

Rydelnik, Michael. *Understanding the Arab-Israeli Conflict*. Chicago: Moody, 2007.

Ryken, Leland, et al., eds. *Dictionary of Biblical Imagery*. Downers Grove: InterVarsity, 1998.

Schmitt, John W., and J. Carl Laney. *Messiah's Coming Temple*. Grand Rapids: Kregel, 1997.

Silva, Moisés. *Philippians*. Baker Exegetical Commentary on the New Testament. Grand Rapids: Baker Academic, 2005.

Smith, Calvin L., ed. *The Jews, Modern Israel and the New Supercessionism: Resources for Christians*. Kent, UK: King's Divinity, 2009.

Smith, Robert. *More Desired than Our Owne Salvation: The Roots of Christian Zionism*. New York: Oxford University Press, 2013.

Stassen, Glen. *Living in the Sermon on the Mount: A Practical Hope for Grace and Deliverance*. San Francisco: Jossey-Bass, 2006.

Tasker, R. V. G. *The Gospel according to Matthew: An Introduction and Commentary*. Tyndale Bible Commentaries. Grand Rapids: Tyndale, 1961.

Teplinsky, Sandra. *Why Care about Israel?* Grand Rapids: Chosen, 2008.

Vlach, Michael J. *Has the Church Replaced Israel? A Theological Evaluation*. Nashville: B & H Academic, 2010.

Bibliography

Waltke, Bruce. "The Kingdom of God in Biblical Theology." In *Looking into the Future: Evangelical Studies in Eschatology*, edited by David W. Baker, 15–27. Grand Rapids: Baker, 2001.

Walton, John. *Genesis*. NIV Application Commentary. Grand Rapids: Zondervan, 2001.

Wenham, Gordon J. *The Book of Leviticus*. New International Commentary of the Old Testament. Grand Rapids: Eerdmans, 1979.

Wright, Bryant. *Seeds of Turmoil: The Biblical Roots of the Inevitable Crisis in the Middle East*. Nashville: Nelson, 2010.

Wright, Christopher. "A Christian Approach to Old Testament Prophecy." In *Jerusalem: Past and Present in the Purposes of God*, edited by P. W. L. Walker, 1–19. Carlisle, UK: Paternoster, 1994.

———. *The Mission of God: Unlocking the Bible's Grand Narrative*. Downers Grove: IVP Academic, 2006.

Wright, N. T. *How God Became King: The Forgotten Story of the Gospels*. New York: HarperOne, 2012.

———. *The New Testament and the People of God*. Minneapolis: Fortress, 1992.

———. *Paul and the Faithfulness of God*. 2 vols. Minneapolis: Fortress, 2013.

———. *Simply Christian: Why Christianity Makes Sense*. San Francisco: HarperSanFrancisco, 2006.

———. *Surprised by Scripture: Engaging Contemporary Issues*. New York: HarperOne, 2014.

42030173R00101

Made in the USA
Lexington, KY
05 June 2015